D1559133

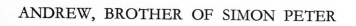

ANDREW, BROTHER OF SIMON PETER

SUPPLEMENTS

TO

NOVUM TESTAMENTUM

EDITORIAL BOARD

VOLUME I

LEIDEN
E. J. BRILL
1958

ANDREW, BROTHER OF SIMON PETER

HIS HISTORY AND HIS LEGENDS

BY

PETER M. PETERSON, Th.D.

LEIDEN
E. J. BRILL
1958

PRINTED IN THE NETHERLANDS

TABLE OF CONTENTS

PREFACE

This is an exhaustive study of the development of the legends about Andrew. The period covered begins with the appearance of the historic Andrew in the Gospel of Mark and ends with the Syriac references to him in the twelfth century. Andrew as patron saint of Scotland is not discussed: first, because the Scottish legend has nothing whatever to do with the stories from the Mediterranean lands; and second, because Scottish research has exhausted the field.

Every attempt has, however, been made to cover Andrew as the hero of the Bible and as the speaker for various Christian groups, such as the Gnostics, in the New Testament Apocrypha. Legends already available in modern language translations are summarized or quoted briefly. The appendix contains two legends for which no full translation has ever been made from the Greek.

This study is dedicated to my wife, Nelly, whose encouragement was a constant source of strength.

CHAPTER ONE

NAME, ORIGIN, CALL.

Andrew, Greek form being *Andréas*, is entirely a Greek name in origin, found as early as Herodotos. [1] That Andrew, like his brother Simon, and like his fellow-disciples, Simon the Zealot and Philip, had Greek names, shows the deep influence of Greek culture even upon simple Galilean fishermen. *Andréas* means "manly"; the etymologies from Semitic by Origen and Jerome [2] are simply learnedness in excess.

Matthew 16 : 18 presents Jesus as calling Simon Peter *"Simon Baryōnā"*. The older writers interpreted this as *Bar-Yōnā*, i.e., Son of Jonah. The Fourth Evangelist misunderstood it as *hyiòs Ioánnou* (1 : 42). From this last arose the Greek legends which gave Simon Peter and Andrew as father *Johánnes* and mother *Johánna*. [3] However, it appears most likely that Andrew's parents must always be unknown to us, for *Baryōnā* written as one word means "extremist, terrorist" [4]. If this is the correct interpretation (as Dr. Cullmann suggests) [5], then either Simon Peter (and Andrew, by implication) were sometime rebels against Rome, or Matthew has confused Simon Peter with Simon the Zealot. As Dr. Cullmann has shown in his book, *Peter*, the Matthaean account of Peter's confession and Jesus' reply is a contamination of Mark 8 : 27-30 and sources peculiar to Matthew. [6] Dr. Cullmann concludes that just as Simon the Zealot (called in Mark and Matthew, *Kananaîos = Qanaiya* = Zealot) was clearly a sometime

---

[1] Article, "Andréas", in PW, vol. 1, 2nd edition, cites Herodotus, VI, 126, for its earliest occurrence: an ancestor of the Athenian tyrant Cleisthenes. Bauer, Walter, *Griechisch-Deutsches Wörterbuch*, 4. Auflage, Berlin: Alfred Töpelmann, 1952, in his article "Andréas" also defends the genuine Greekness of the name.

[2] The text of both Origen and Jerome is given in PL 23, pp. 1171-3.

[3] Schermann, *Vitae*, p. 202 = *Corpus Scriptorum Historiae Byzantinorum*, Chronicon Paschale, vol. II, p. 142.

[4] Dalman, Gustav H., *Aramäisch-Neuhebräisches Wörterbuch*, 3. unveränderte Auflage, 1938. So Eisler, Robert, *Jesous basileus ou basileusas*, 1929, p. 67 who follows Eliezer ben Jehuda, *Thesaurus totius hebraitatis*, cited by Cullmann, Oscar, *Peter: Disciple-Apostle-Martyr*, translated by Floyd V. Filson: London and Philadelphia, 1953, p. 22, note 23.

[5] Cullmann, *op. cit.*, pp. 21-22.

[6] *Ibid.*, pp. 170-184.

1

anti-Roman, so probably were Simon and Andrew. This is an entirely reasonable conclusion, since Galilee was notorious for its rebellious fanatics. On the other hand, since Matthew was composed in Greek from Greek sources, the author may not have understood the Aramaic technical terms left Hellenized but untranslated in his sources and so came to the false conclusion that a certain Simon Baryōnā was to be identified with his familiar Simon Peter rather than the "Canaanite" Simon. As a general rule, deeds or things of the less important people are in the end attributed to familiar heroes or villains. Such was the case with Goliath of Gath, whose slayer in 2 Samuel 21 : 19 was Elhanan, while 1 Samuel 17 tells the more familiar story of David killing Goliath. Other examples of erroneous identification of the familiar in place of the unfamiliar will be mentioned later.

The parentage of Andrew is, in any event, unknown to us; however, his call to discipleship, Mark 1 : 16-18, tells how Jesus " "passing by the Sea of Galilee, saw Simon and Andrew, Simon's brother, casting a net into the sea, for they were fishermen. And Jesus said to them, "Follow me, and I will make you fishers of men". And, immediately leaving their nets behind, they followed him" ". Matthew 4 : 18-22 merely changes the word order a little but still mentions Andrew. Luke 5 : 1-11 tells quite a different story, omitting any mention of Andrew whatever and replacing him with "the two sons of Zebedee, James and John, Simon's partners."

Luke-Acts mention Andrew only in the lists of the Twelve (Luke 6 : 12-16 and Acts 1 : 13). Matthew mentions Andrew only in the story above and in his list of the Twelve (10 : 2-4). Mark 3 : 16-19, of course, gives a list of the Twelve including Andrew, too. Yet Mark in two other episodes mentions Andrew by name, while Matthew and Luke in their retelling of both stories omit Andrew entirely. That both evangelists independently omitted Andrew's name from their rewrites of Mark shows clearly that Andrew as disciple (or for that matter, as apostle) was historically a person of no importance whatsoever.

Mark implies that Andrew and Peter came from Capernaum, a village on the northwest shore of the Sea of Galilee. 1 : 21 reads : "And they went into Capernaum; and immediately on the sabbath he entered the synagogue and taught". Jesus' teaching created excitement, to all of which Andrew was apparently a witness, for verses 29-31 mention him by name. "Immediately, having left the synagogue, they entered the house of Simon and of Andrew, with James and

John. Now Simon's mother-in-law lay fevered, and immediately they told him of her. And coming, having took her up by the hand, he raised her up; and the fever left her, and she served them." Matthew 8 : 14-15 and Luke 4 : 38-39, among other improvements in Mark's clumsy Greek, omit the names "Andrew, with James and John."

Andrew is not referred to again in Mark, until on that fatal trip to Jerusalem Jesus leaves the temple and the city. Mark 13 : 3-4 tells us that as Jesus was "Sitting on the Mount of Olives opposite the temple, Rock and James and John and Andrew asked him privately, saying 'Tell us, when will this be, and what will be the sign when these things are all to be accomplished?' " Jesus replies with his famous apocalyptic prediction of the destruction of Jerusalem and perhaps of this world.

CHAPTER TWO

THE FOURTH GOSPEL

The Gospel attributed to John presents quite a different picture.
Here is Andrew presented as a personality who can be quoted,
described, and consulted in his own right. The scene of the first
incident is John's preaching and baptizing at Bethany beyond the
Jordan. (1 : 35-44) "The next day again John was standing with
two of his disciples, and looking at Jesus as he walked, he said, 'There
is God's lamb!' And the two disciples heard him speaking and followed Jesus. But Jesus, having turned and saw them following him, said
to them, 'What are you looking for?' And they said to him, 'Rabbi
(which means Teacher), where are you staying?' He said to them,
'Come and see'. They went then, and saw where he was staying,
and with him they stayed that day, for it was about the tenth hour.
Andrew, Simon Rock's brother was one of the two who heard John
speak and followed him. He first found his own brother, Simon, and
said to him, 'We have found the Messiah' (which means Anointed).
He took him to Jesus. Looking at him, Jesus said, 'You are Simon,
son of John? You shall be called Cephas' (which means Rock).
The next day he decided to leave for Galilee, and sought out Philip.
Jesus said to him, 'Come and see'. Now Philip was from Bethsaida,
the city of Rock and Andrew."

The contrast between Mark and John is striking. Andrew and
Peter are no longer fishermen by the northwest Galilean shore, but
disciples of John at Bethany on the eastern side of the Jordan. Where
before Jesus had called himself to Andrew and Simon to become his
disciples, now the Baptist identifies Jesus to Andrew and an unknown
fellow-disciple of the Baptist. Andrew goes and later brings Peter.
As mentioned above, the *baryōnā* became a son of John (*Yōhānān,
Iōánnēs*). Bethsaida has replaced Capernaum as Andrew's city of origin;
indeed Bethsaida is flatly identified as the "city" of Philip, Andrew,
and Peter. Since Bethsaida is but a few miles from Capernaum on
the north shore of the Sea of Galilee, this tradition lies well within
the range of probability.

In the feeding of the Five Thousand (John 6 : 5-14, cf. Mark 6 :
32-44 and 8 : 1-10, Matthew 14 : 13-21 and 15 : 32-39, Luke 9 : 11-17)

4

the former of the Marcan doublets is expanded. Andrew tells Jesus, "There is a lad here who has five barley loaves and two fish; but what are they among so many?" The unknown disciple of Mark 6 is here identified with Philip; Andrew's question has no precise parallel in the Synoptics.

Of more importance is the story of the Greeks' coming to Jesus (John 12 : 20-34), for Andrew now appears in a position of authority. The Greeks "went to Philip, the one from Bethsaida of Galilee, and asked him, 'Sir, we want to see Jesus.' Philip went and told Andrew. Andrew and Philip went and told Jesus."

In the Fourth Gospel, Andrew is placed in a position of leadership. From the Johannine version of the Call, the Byzantine Church found its title *Prōtóklētos*, the First-Called, to give their hero, St. Andrew. [1]

---

[1] Gedeōn, Manouēl I., *Patriarchikoi Pinikes*, Thessalonikē, 1889, pp. 81-89, for example, almost invariably uses the designation prōtoklētos for Andrew. So, too, the Greek abridgments of the Andrew Passion in Bonnet,, *Sup*. Laudatio, p. 3, 1. 4; Narratio, p. 47, 13. Bonnet, *Acta*, p. 1, 1.7 variant in the longer Greek version of the Epistle and p. 220, 1.8 variant in Martyrium Matthiae. Schermann, *Vitae*, Mēnologion b., p. 186, 1.10 and c., p. 195, 1.4. The short Mēnologion of a modern Greek massbook, *Hē Theia Leitourgia*, Athens, Michael I. Saliberou, no date, p. 140 gives simply the title "Andrew, the Prōtóklētos and Apostle."

CHAPTER THREE

ANDREW AND THE "ACTS" AMONG THE CHURCH FATHERS, UP TO 500

Before discussing the age and origin of the various "Acts of Andrew", let us first consider the references to the First-Called Apostle in the Church Fathers up to the ninth century. The following is an exhaustive listing of all Latin, Greek, Syriac, Coptic, and one Gothic, mentionings of the Apostle Andrew outside the longer "lives" of him collected by Bonnet, James, Hennecke, Budge, Lewis, and Malan.

The Gospel of Peter (usually dated as about 150) [1] is a contamination of the canonic four Gospels and the unknown author's Docetic, if not Gnostic, theology. Serapion of Antioch (c. 190) [2] already attacks it for its Docetism. The surviving fragment is very small and gives us really only a hint of how its author used (like the Fourth Evangelist) the other apostles to bolster his story. The conclusion, however, (clearly based on John 21) will show something of the nature of the story. "But I, Simon Peter, and my brother Andrew took our nets and went to the sea; and with us was Levi the son of Alphaeus, whom the Lord..."

This is the only mention of either Andrew or Levi in the fragment which has come down to us. Unfortunately, like so much of the literature of the early church the Gospel of Peter is bitterly anti-Jewish, a tendency which poisons apocryphal acts and gospels far more than the canonic.

The Epistle of the Apostles, written perhaps about 160 in Asia Minor [3], is a quite uninteresting more or less orthodox pamphlet

---

[1] James, Montague Rhodes, *The Apocryphal New Testament*, Oxford, 1924, pp. 90-1. The Greek can be found in Harnack, Adolf, *Bruchstücke des Evangeliums und Apokalypse des Petrus*, TU IX, 2, section 60; or p. 8, in number 3 of Hans Lietzmann, *Kleine Texte*: *Apocrypha I* edited by Erich Klostermann, Bonn, 1903.

[2] Serapion of Antioch is quoted by Eusebios, *Ecclesiastic History*, book VI, section 12. The best edition is Schwart's in *Die Griechischen Christlichen Schriftsteller der Ersten Drei Jahrhunderte*, Kirchenväterliche Kommission = PG 20. Cf. James, *op. cit.*, pp. 13 and 90.

[3] Lacau, Pierre und Schmidt, Carl, *Gespräche Jesu mit Seinen Jüngern nach der Auferstehung*, TU, III. Reihe, vol. 13, = James, *op. cit.*, pp. 485-403. These are more complete than Lacau's earlier *Fragments d'apocryphes coptes*, vol. 9 of *Mémoires publiés... de l'Institut Français d'Archéologie Orientale*, Cairo, 1904.

in which Jesus answers questions of the Apostles in lengthy and un-realistic form. It survives completely in Ethiopic, and in Coptic and Latin fragments. It is quoted by Clement of Alexandria (died c. 215) as "Scripture" and the *Apostolic Constitutions* (earliest form c. 250, quotation in form of c. 400). The writing is distinctly anti-Docetic, as the following passage (also the only one in which Andrew is involved as an individual) shows: "Peter, put your finger in the print of the nails in my hands and you, too, Thomas, put your finger into the wound of the spear in my side; but you, Andrew, look on my feet and see whether they press the earth; for it is written in the prophet: "A phantom of a devil makes no footprint on the earth." The anti-Docetism interpretation of John 20 : 27 is largely based on this passage. As for the prophet above quoted, no one knows. Harnack suggests Wisdom of Solomon 18 : 17 while Guerrier suggests Daniel 14 : 18 ff. Commodian of Gaza (c. 250?) quotes the passage as *"Vesti-gium umbra non facit."* (Shades leave no traces). [1]

The Muratorian Fragment, which may date from the end of the second century, credits Andrew in part for the Gospel of John. "On the same night, it was revealed to Andrew of the Apostles that, all [the Apostles] knowing, John should describe in his own name all the facts." [2]

Origen (died 254), in one of his occasional excessive interpretations of Scripture attempts to give the etymology of Andrew's name. He explains it as "fitting power, or the answerer". [3] In a lost passage, cited by Eusebius, Origen gives the mission field of the Apostles, "Andrew (receiving) the Scythians." [4] This is the oldest passage which bears the influence of the Acts of Andrew and *Matthias*. Stachys, who (in legends later than the ninth century), is called a disciple of Andrew, is in Origen's *Commentary to Romans* 16 : 9 simply called "with Ampliatus, a participant in the apostolic work." [5]

After Origen's monumental work, especially in Old Testament, Gnostic writings take a more orthodox character. At least one text coming down to us fully recognizes the value of the Old Testament, even if the treatment is allegoric in order to bring the Older Covenant

---

[1] Lacau und Schmidt, *op. cit.*, pp. 42-43 and 221. James, *op. cit.*, pp. 485-486.
[2] Text from Vögel, Heinrich Joseph, *Grundriss der Einleitung in das Neue Testament*, Münster, 1925, appendix, p. III. A modernized Latin text is found in *Encheiridon Biblicum*, Rome, 1955, pp. 1 f. Both in Hans Lietzmann's *Kleine Texte*, number 1.
[3] PL 23, pp. 1171-1173.
[4] Eusebios, *Ecclesiastic History*, book III, section 1.
[5] Origen, PG 14, p. 1281A, book X, section 23.

into the Gnostic thinking. This is the famous *Pistis Sophia*, of which
the present form is from the second half of the third century. [1] The
book is written in the common Hellenistic-Byzantine style which
has the hero (here, the resurrected Jesus) answer at great length the
questions of His Apostles whose questions are short and whose
replies are mere biblical quotations. Only Mary Magdalene appears,
in any way, as a personality; of the Twelve, only Peter, Thomas,
Andrew, and the sons of Zebedee are allowed to ask questions.
The artificiality of the book is well shown in the following selection.

"Andrew stept up and spoke, 'My Lord, concerning the solution
of the sixth repentance of the Pistis Sophia, Thy enlightening Power
first prophesied through David in the 129th Psalm, wherein (the Power)
said: (He quotes the De profundis, vss. 3-8, LXX 129, Heb. 130)'.

Jesus spoke to him 'Well said, Andrew, you blessed one, this is
the solution of repentance. Amen, amen, I say to you, I will perfect
you in all mysteries of Light, and in all knowledges (gnosis) from the
Inner of the Inner unto the Outer of the Outer......' " [2] Although
clearly written originally in Greek, the book survives only in Coptic;
surprisingly enough, it leaves no trace of itself in the later Coptic
or Ethiopic literature which concerns the very late Apocryphal
Acts of the Apostles.

Eusebios (died 340), in his Ecclesiastic History, has left two
comments on Andrew. The first, a citation from Origen, simply
mentions that Andrew had a mission in Scythia; the second, that
"the writings circulated among the heretics" include those of Andrew.[3]

Philastrius, the second Paul of his age, (died 387 as bishop of Brescia)
complains in his Book on Heresies that "The apocrypha of the Blessed
Andrew the Apostle are Manichaean, i.e., the Acts which he made
coming from Pontus to Greece, which were written then by later
disciples of the Apostles, from whom the Manichaeans have obtained
them and others similar to those of Andrew, the Acts of John the
Evangelist, and of Blessed Peter the Apostle, in which they made
great miracles and wonders so that cattle, dogs and beasts speak and
have human souls. Really, those who think dogs and cattle are like
that are damned heretics!" [4] The enthusiastic missionary and bishop

---

[1] *Die Pistis Sophia*, edited and translated by Carl Schmidt, in *Koptisch-Gnostische
Schriften*, 1. Band, in *die Griechischen Christlichen Schriftsteller*, Kirchenväterliche
Kommission, 1905, p. XVII. Schmidt agrees with the earlier dating of Harnack.
[2] *Ibid.*, p. 48.
[3] Eusebios, *op. cit.*, book III, section 1.
[4] Philasterius, *de Haeresibus*, ch. 88 in PL 12.

makes here the first clear reference to the Acts of Andrew which does *not* mention the Scynthian mission, but the events leading up to the death of Andrew.

Gregory of Nazianus (died 389 or 390) simply states that "Andrew to Epirus" (went) [1] and that there are feast days honoring martyrs like Andrew [2]. His Western contemporary, Pacian (died 390) is said to have stated that the Montanists had nothing to do with Andrew as they claimed [3]. This statement is the only indication that the Montanists (whose main emphasis was on their possession of the gift of prophecy rather than a literary tradition) made use of any literature concerning Andrew.

Epiphanios (died c. 403) in his *Panarion* [4] is often wrongly quoted in regard to the concept of a corpus of five apocryphal acts attributed to Leucios among which is the book attributed to Andrew. He states that the early heretics "were often opposed by the holy John and his companions, Leucios and many others". Because so many ancient authors, those cited above and Photios later, called the author of the apocryphal corpus of acts used by the Manichaeans by the name of Leucios, this passage, which is the only other Greek mention of Leucios, is cited as the identification of Leucios. However, as several more recent commentators (Lake, Hennecke, James) have pointed out, the Leucios of Epiphanios is a refuter of heretics. Therefore, they say, Leucios was considered to be the author of the apocryphal Acts of John; and only later, by error, he was given credit for the whole of the Manichaean corpus. This theory is probably right; but I would make the reservation that Leucios was so regarded by the Manichaeans of the West and therefore is not cited by the Fathers of the East, as one of the founders of the Manichaeans. Photios, I suspect, took his information from a Latin, rather than a Greek, source, since he is the only Eastern Doctor who mentions a Leucian authorship for the Acts of Andrew.

John Chrysostom (died c. 407) seems to have had a most sceptical view of the whole apocryphal literature and even to some extent of the relics of his own time. Altho Jerome (see below) and others definitely date the bringing of the relics of Andrew, Luke, and Timothy

---

[1] Gregory of Nazianzos, *Oratio* 33 in PG 36, p. 228.

[2] Gregory of Nazianzos, *Oratio* 4 in PG 35, p. 589.

[3] Cited by Lake, Kirsopp in "Acts (Apocryphal)", *Dictionary of the Apostolic Church*, edited by Hastings, 1915. This is the only reference by Lake which I have been unable to locate.

[4] Book 51, section 6.

to Constantinople in 357 at the order of the Emperor Constantius'
Chrysostom nevertheless comments in a sermon: "But, at least for
most of them, we do not know where the bones of the Apostles
lie. For the graves of Peter and Paul and John and Thomas are famous,
but concerning the rest, where they are, no one is at all cognizant." [1]

The Gothic Calendar (attributed to Ufilas, died c. 381, but possibly
later) gives 30 November as the date for Andrew the Apostle [2].
Unfortunately the Arian as well as the Catholic literature of the Goths
has perished except for fragments of the calendar and the Bible. The
ancient Carthaginian Calendar gives a date on or before the Kalends
of December but the number has fallen out. [3] So late is any reference
to Andrew's day of death.

A probably spurious sermon which is attributed to Athanasius
(died 373) but which may be from the fifth century simply states that
"Andrew preached and was crucified in Greece." [4]

Jerome (died 420) vigorously defended the relics and worship
of the saints. In his letter to Marcellus, he states that Andrew was in
Achaia. [5]

In one defense, *Against Vigilantius*, he exclaims, "Are we sacrilegious to go to the churches of the Apostles? Was Constantius the
Emperor sacrilegious when he brought the holy relics of Andrew,
Luke and Timothy to Constantinople?" [6] Elsewhere he gives the
date "in the twentieth year of Constantius" [7] i.e., 357. The *Martyrologium Romanum* still celebrates the event on 9 May.

To Origen's (see above) fabulous etymology of Andrew's name,
Jerome added the phrase "of a violent character". [8]

Evodius of Uzala (died 424) twice gives us the first extensive
quotations from the Acts of Andrew. "Observe, in the Acts of Leucios
which he wrote under the name of the Apostles, what manner of
things you (Manichaeans) accept about Maximilla the wife of Egetes:
who, refusing to pay her due to her husband—altho the Apostle

---

[1] *Homily on the Epistle to the Hebrews*, number 26, section 2. PG 63, p. 179.

[2] PL 18, p. 878 f.

[3] PG 13, p. 1227.

[4] PG 28, pp. 1101-8.

[5] *Ad Marcellum*, PL 22, p. 589. (cf. Lipsius, *Ap.*, I, p. 608).

[6] *Contra Vigilantium*, ch. 5 in PL 23, p. 313 or in *Hieronymus I* of *Bibliothek der
Kirchenväter*, translated by Ludwig Schade, Munich, 1914, p. 308. (Cf. Lipsius,
Ap., I, p. 607.)

[7] *De Viris Illustribus*, PL 23, ch. 7 at end, p. 122. Cf. Socrates, *Ecclesiastic
History*, book I, ch. 40, PG 57. (Cf. Lipsius, *Ap.*, I, p. 607).

[8] See footnote 2, p. 1.

(Paul) said, (I Corinthians 7 : 3) 'The husband must give his wife what is due her and the wife must do the same by her husband'— imposed her maid Euclia upon her husband and fixed her up, as is there written, with hostile attractions and paintings, and substituted her in her own place at night, so that he used her in his ignorance as his wife. There is also written, that when this same Maximilla and Iphidamia were gone together to hear the Apostle Andrew, a beautiful child, who, Leucios would have us understand, was either God or at least an angel, went with them to the Apostle Andrew and went to the praetorium of Egetes, and entering their chamber imitated a woman's voice, Maximilla's, complaining of the sufferings of women-kind, and Iphidamia's replying. When Egetes heard this dialog, he went away."

Evodius quotes another sentence, which is similar to those found in the Vatican manuscript-fragment of the Acts of Andrew: "In the Acts written by Leucios, which the Manichaeans accept, one reads 'For the deceitful fictions and pretended exhibitions and the compulsion of visible things proceed not from their own nature but from man who voluntarily has worsened himself through seduction.'"[1]

Augustine (died 430) was also a bitter opponent of the Manichae-ans, to whose religion he himself once belonged. In his *Against Felix*, he wrote "You have placed (in a high place) the Acts written by Leucios, just as if they were written as (true) Acts of Apostles."[2]

Socrates (his book ends with 439) wrote a continuation of Eusebios' Ecclesiastic History, in which he makes the first mention of Argyropo-lis possessing a bishop, but no mention of Andrew, who according to later sources, was supposed to have stayed there two years and to have ordained Stachys as first bishop of Byzantium. Socrates[3] also calls Metrophanes "first bishop of Byzantium". Proclos (died 446)[4] and Hesychios (died 440)[5] tell nothing of Andrew's mission or death. This is important for the argument *ex silentio* later.

Eucherius of Lyons (died 450)[6] simply states in a listing of the Apostles "Andrew with preaching softened Scythia". His contempo-

---

[1] *De Fide contra Manichaeos*, PL 42, ch. 5, p. 1141 and ch. 38, p. 1150. Cf. James, *op. cit.*, pp. 349 f. Hennecke I, pp. 459, 463 and II, pp. 356, 549f. Lipsius, *Ap.*, I, pp. 543, 564, 590ff., 602.

[2] Book 2, ch. 6, in PL 42, p. 509.

[3] Socrates, *Ecclesiastic History*, book I, ch. 37 and VII, ch. 25 in PG 57.

[4] PG 65, pp. 821-8.

[5] PG 93, pp. 1477-80.

[6] *Instructiones ad Salonium*, PL 50, p. 809.

rary, Peter Chrysologus of Ravenna (died 450) made a long sermon
on Andrew's birthday. Unfortunately, the date is unknown; just
when Andrew was born is no where else mentioned among the fathers.
The sermon is mostly in praise of sainthood as such, the only information that is new for us being: "Andrew that Blessed one, is
rightly believed born today, for not for this life did he come forth
from his mother's womb.... Peter climbed a cross, Andrew a tree,
and as they desired, they became co-sufferers with Christ." [1]

Theodoretus of Cyprus (died 460) in his *Commentary on Psalm 116*
tells us "So too the divine Andrew enlightened Greece with rays of
knowledge of God." [2] In the West, Turribus of Astorga (died 460)
repeats in substance the theory of the Leucian authorship of the Acts
of Andrew. "It is manifest that all apocryphal books are either
forgeries or just impossible, especially those attributed to Saint
Andrew and those attributed to Saint John, which Leucios with his
sacrilegious mouth forged." [3] A little later, the Pope Gelasius (died
496) condemned "The Acts under the name of Andrew the Apostle"
and "all books made by Leucios, disciple of the devil." [4] Some attribute the Gelasian decree to the sixth century, but since the list is
made by readers of Jerome and Epiphanios and not by readers of the
apocryphal works themselves, it seems to me to be an unimportant
point. Another proponent, in one form, is Innocent I who in a letter
in 405 to Exsuperbius, also suggests a Leucian origin of the Acts of
Andrew. [5]

Up to now, the traditions of the fathers concerning the Apostle
Andrew can be summarized as follows:

1) That Andrew has his mission in Scythia, in Origen as cited by
   Eusebius, and repeated by Eucherius of Lyons.

2) That Andrew was in Achaia, Epirus, or "Greece" is stated by
   Philastrius, Gregory of Nazianzus, (Pseudo-) Athanasias, Jerome,
   Evodius, and Theodoretos.

3) That Andrew was elsewhere, e.g., with John (in Ephesus?), is
   found in the *Muratorian Fragment*.

---

[1] *Oratio* 133, PL 52, pp. 563-4.
[2] PG 80, p. 1805 bottom (Cf. Lipsius, *Ap.*, I, p. 608).
[3] PL 54 (not PL 50, as usually stated, so erroneously in Index to PL) p. 694
(Cf. Lipsius, *Ap.*, I, 543 f. *passim*).
[4] Hennecke II, p. 356. James, *op. cit.*, p. 22.
[5] Hennecke, II, pp. 355-6, Lake, *op. cit.*

4) No statement at all on his mission, is to be found in Gospel of
Peter, Epistle of the Apostles, *Pistis Sophia*, John Chrysostom, the
Gothic and Carthaginian Calendars, Socrates, Proclos, Hesychios,
and the author(s) of the Gelasian decree. The year 500 shows as
yet the traditions concerning the Apostle (outside the yet undiscus-
sed Acts of Andrew and Acts of Andrew and Matthias) were
quite unsettled. Only a mistaken tradition of a Leucian corpus of
apocryphal acts, including one or more attributed to or about
Andrew can be shown to be current.

CHAPTER FOUR

TRADITIONS IN THE WEST AFTER 500

Beginning with Gregory of Tours (died 595) and his contemporaries, Venantius Fortunatus (died c. 600) and Isidor of Sevilla (died 636), the traditions in the West reach a fixed and permanent form. The apparent source is Gregory. Just before he died, the pious and credulous bishop made a summary of the Acts of Andrew and of the Acts of Andrew and Matthias. This will be discussed later in the section on the Acts. In one of his earlier writings, however, Gregory (in his usual confused style) states that Andrew suffered at Patrae in Achaia, that his church is there, and that after his death manna and oil came from his tomb. Gregory tells also of a Mammolus in Justinian's time (527-565) who went to Andrew's tomb to be cured of his inability to urinate. The Saint answered his prayers and the (un)fortunate man urinated a colossal stone. [1]

His contemporary, Venantius Fortunatus, left a poem-list of the apostles, in which "Noble Achaia sent her Andrew to die". [2] Isidor of Sevilla felt less poetic and gave the world a list of the Apostles and their fates. According to Isidor, "Andrew, which means noble (decorus), Peter's brother , was according to John the first, according to Matthew the second from the first, [to be called]. He accepted his lot-given preaching-fields Scythia and Achaia, in whose city of Patrae itself he died, suspended from a cross." [3]

The anonymous *Breviarium Apostolorum* gives virtually the same information. "Andrew, which means manly (virilis) or noble (decorus) was Peter's brother. He preached in Scythia (variant : Spasiam!) and Achaia and there in Patrae, a city, he died suspended from a cross on the 30 November." [4]

The Brevarium Gothicum of the Mozarabic Liturgy tells a similar story in prose and hymn: "Andrew, because he preached the mystery

---

[1] *Glory of the Martyrs' Miracles*, book I, ch. 3 in PL 71, paragraphs 754, 756, and 810.

[2] Schermann, *Vitae*, p. 215 = PL 88, p. 270.

[3] Schermann, *Propheten*, p. 249, under symbol Li. (Cf. Lipsius *Ap.* I, 609).

[4] Schermann, *ibid.*, under symbol Lb. and *Vitae*, p. 207 f. (Cf. Lipsius, *Ap.*, I, 212, 609).

of the Cross, deserved to die on the fork-shaped cross (crucis...
patibulum)... He preached in Achaia and there was [crucified] by
Aegaeas (*sic*). " [1]

A large number of anonymous manuscripts collected by Schermann
tells in extremely brief form Andrew's death and or burial place.
The titles are given below in single quotation marks ('), the text in
double quotation marks (").

1) 'Notices of Places of the Holy Apostles': "The 2 December is
   the feast day of St. Andrew the Apostle in the city of Patrae in
   the province of Achaia."
2) 'A certain Laterculus, otherwise unknown': "Andrew was buried
   in Patrae, a city of Achaia".
3) 'Notices of Regions and Cities in which the Venerable Bodies of
   the Holy Apostles and Evangelists Rest': "Andrew the Apostle
   rests in Patrae, a city in the province of Achaia."
4) 'Verses to be memorized': "St. Andrew among the Achivi"
   (*sic*) did die.
5) 'In which Place each Apostle Lies': "Andrew in Patrae".
6) 'The Apostles Divide the Mission Field by Lot': "Andrew draws
   Scythia." [2]

It would be quite in place here to quote the *Martyrologium Romanum*.

"30 November is at Patrae of Achaia the feast day of St. Andrew
the Apostle, who preached the Gospel of Christ in Thrace and
Scythia. He was arrested by Aegeas the Proconsul, at first locked in
prison, then most gravely cut, and finally suspended from a cross.
On it, he lived on for two days, teaching the people; and having
asked the Lord that he not be taken down from the cross, he was
surrounded with a great splendor from Heaven, while a light shortly
shown, and he gave up the ghost." [3]

Each of these texts, it should be remembered, came as a part of a
list of the Twelve. The text of Isidor and the *Breviárium Apostolorum*

---

[1] PL 86, pp. 1263 f.
[2] Schermann, *Vitae*, 1. on p. 212, 1.3.
                2. on p. 213.
                3. on p. 214, 1. 10
                4. on p. 215.
                5. on p. 216.
                6. on p. 217.
[3] Edition in *Propylaeum ad Acta Sanctorum Decembris*, Brussels, 1940. cf. *Epistle
of the Presbyters and Deacons* in Bonnet, *Acta*, pp. 32-34 and *Passio* in Bonnet,
Sup., pp. 69-70.

is possibily dependent upon a Latin version of the Graeco-Syriac Text given in the next section. The *Martyrologium Romanum* is based upon these lists of the Twelve and upon the Acts of Andrew and the Acts of Andrew and Matthias, as will be evident from the second half of this book.

James [1] cites a late apocryphon which quotes a section of the Acts of Andrew: "When, finally Andrew also had come to a wedding, he too, to manifest the glory of God, disjoined certain who were intended to marry each other, men and women, and instructed them to continue holy in the single state."

In summary, the Latin sources (outside Gregory's Book of St. Andrew's Miracles) emphasize

1) a Scythian mission, as found earlier in Eusebios and in the Andrew-Matthias legend;
2) a mission, crucifixion, and death in Patrae of Achaia at the hands of Aegeas;
3) while most sources depend upon mere lists of the twelve or liturgic formulas, at least one Latin version (cf. the immediately above cited apocryphon) of the original Acts in its most Encratitic form still circulated.

---

[1] *Op. cit.*, p. 349.

CHAPTER FIVE

TRADITIONS IN THE EAST, GREEK AND SYRIAC, AFTER 500

For this section, I am relying greatly upon Schermann's publication of the texts and partly upon his commentary. But to his collection of pseudonymous and anonymous texts, I add a few texts from known and datable Byzantine fathers. Probably the oldest of the later lists of the Apostles and Disciples of the Lord is the Syriac text found in Codex Sinaiticus Syrus 10, whose handwriting is of the ninth century but whose origin is probably directly from a sixth century source. It reads concerning Andrew and Stachys simply: "Andrew, Simon's brother, died in the city Patrae." After the Twelve is found a list of "The Names of the Seventy Apostles, Composed by Irenaeus, Bishop of Lyon," and some "Six More were with Peter of Caesarea", which includes as sixty-first: "Stachys." [1]

Probably also from the sixth century is a Greek translation of a Syriac text similar to the above, but by someone cognizant of the Acts of Andrew, which gives the simple statement: "Andrew, Simon Peter's brother, having preached in Greece, at Patrae was killed by Aegeates." [2]

Theophanes Cerameus (died 817) made a long sermon in praise of Andrew, based in part on some version of the Acts of Andrew and Matthias as well as the Acts of Andrew. His version of the latter is reminiscent of Peter Chrysologus' sermon on Andrew in that it also mentions his death on a tree. "All you listeners know how the great [Andrew] stayed first at Sinope and later at Patrae; and how those wild men lept upon him and tore the Apostle's body with their teeth. In Achaia, however, where he preached the Gospel, he did not avoid being brought like the Lord to the cross (*stauros*). Aegeates, Our Savior's enemy..... crucified the great Apostle on an olive tree (*déndron elaías*)." [3] The rest of the sermon is simply a comment on sainthood in general and the Johannine Gospel in particular.

About the same time (altho Schermann would date it earlier),

---

[1] Schermann, *Vitae*, pp. 218-220; *Propheten*, p. 250.
[2] Schermann, *Vitae*, p. 171; *Propheten*, p. 249.
[3] PG 94, p. 904. Cf. Lipsius, *Ap.*, I, 605.

17

another Byzantine wished to change the legends about Andrew. Pseudo-Epiphanios, as he is now called, was the first to introduce into the stories about Andrew or the Twelve the statement that he appointed Stachys the first bishop for Byzantium. His reference to an older tradition is primarily to the Acts and his organization is based on the Graeco-Syriac text just quoted above. The passages pertinent to Andrew read: "Andrew, however, his (Peter's) brother, as they have handed down the tradition to us, preached to the Scythians and Sogdianians and the Gorsinians and in great Sevastopol, where is the castle Apsaros and Lake Hyssos and the River Phasis. From there (he went to where) the Ethiopians dwell, but is buried in Patrae of Achaia, having been tied to a cross by Aegeas (*sic*), King of Patrae... Philip... was from Bethsaida, from the village of Peter and Andrew.... (Luke's body) was transferred last to Constantinople with Andrew's and Timothy's...... Stachys whom Paul mentioned in the same Epistle (Romans 16 : 9) was appointed first bishop of Byzantium by Andrew the Apostle in Argyropolis of Thrace..... Philogos, whom also Paul mentioned (v. 15) was made bishop of Sinope by Andrew." [1]

In the present texts of Nicephoros Callistos (died 826) a similar story is found. Altho there is some reason to doubt the passages, they do form a basis for attempting to date the Pseudo-Epiphanian forgery and for that reason I quote the points of Andrew's non-Biblic life as recorded in the Nicephoros Callistos which has come down to us. "Andrew was chosen by lot (*klērōi*) to go to the heathen.... Having visited Cappadocia, Galatia, and Bythinia, he went to the city of the cannibals in Scythia's desert on the other side of the Black Sea, going north and east from Byzantium... where he made Stachys the first bishop.... then thru Thrace, Macedonia, Thessaly, and Achaia, he traveled...... Andrew was crucified by Aegeates the proconsul.... because his wife Maximilla and his brother Stratocles went to Christ." [2]

A worthy successor to Pseudo-Epiphanios is the famous forgery known as Pseudo-Dorotheos or Pseudo-Procopios. Altho full of the most amazing anachronisms, it is still quoted extensively by Greek Orthodox scholars as the main proof that Andrew ordained the first bishop of Constantinople. Its literary influence is such that all later

---

[1] Schermann, *Vitae*, pp. 108 f., 1. 7 ff.; *Propheten*, p. 249. See Lipsius, *Ap.*, I, pp. 193 ff, 203, *passim*.

[2] PG 145, p. 860 f. Cf. *Acts of Andrew and Matthias*, 1, 1. Lipsius, *Ap.*, I, pp. 189, 570, 608 ff.

texts bear its influence, whether in Greek or in Syriac, while a modern scholar lists it among the pseudepigraphs of the New Testament. The alleged author is Dorotheos of Tyre, who is said by the forger to have died about 361; the translator claims to have done his work in 525; the absence of any reference to the villain of the story (one Zeuxippos) until after Nicephoros Callistos, shows that the composition is from the first half of the ninth century, at the earliest. Photios (see below) had no mention at all, either of Pseudo-Epiphanios or of Pseudo-Dorotheos; so perhaps the dating is later. The Photian controversy, however, seems the likely period to have inspired such a document. [1] The most original part of the document is here given.

"For Andrew, having crossed the Pontus, came to preach Christ to the Byzantines. At that time, a blood-thirsty man, Zeuxippos, was ruler. He used to ask foreigners, upon their arrival in Byzantium, about the Christ, before he would permit them to enter the city. If anyone confessed Christ, (Zeuxippos) ordered him bound hand and foot with chains and to be sunk into the sea. Hearing this and sailing around Byzantium, Andrew settled in that part of Thrace nearest Byzantium, at one stadion's distance, in Argyropolis for a period of two years, during which he established a congregation of truth-loving and law-abiding men. As soon as he had some two thousand in the congregation, he erected an altar to Christ, and ordained Stachys as bishop." [2] Pseudo-Epiphanios is also quoted word for word, but no credit is given to any author other than Dorotheos, bishop of Tyre. [3]

Photios, who was Patriarch at Constantinople from 858 to 867 and again from 878 until his death in 886, ignored the two forgeries mentioned above, if indeed, they actually existed in his time. The learned Patriarch, in his famous, and oft-quoted, *Bibliotheca*, left us a criticism of the Acts of Andrew, which, in my opinion, may be based in part on Latin as well as Greek commentators. "One reads the book called the Travels of the Apostles (*períodoi*) with certain Acts (*práxeis*) of Peter, John, Andrew, Thomas and Paul, but, as the book itself makes clear, Leucios Charinos wrote them." [4] Since Photios is the only

---

[1] Schermann, *Vitae*, pp. XLI-XLV; *Propheten*, pp. 182-7.

[2] Schermann, *Vitae*, pp. 146 f.

[3] *Ibid.*, pp. 153-7. cf. pp. 108 f. (Cf. Lipsius, *Ap.* I, *passim* as listed in Ergänzungsband, p. 136).

[4] PG 103, p. 389, "codex" 114.

Greek writer to mention Leucios in connection with the Acts, I suspect that one or more of the texts in his possession were a Latin-commentated version or he used one of the Latin fathers quoted earlier. That Photios *could* have possessed one of the originally Gnostic-Docetic texts of the Acts, is shown by a statement made by Pseudo-Dorotheos: "We find in the historic compositions of the divine Dorotheos that Simon the Cyrenaean was crucified instead of the Christ." [1]

Following the path of the Epiphanian-Dorothean forgeries, rather than Photios' implied condemnation, was the latter's younger contemporary, Niketas David of Paphlago, (died c. 894?). In a lengthy sermon, which deals primarily with Andrew's actions in the Fourth Gospel, he mentions some new names in the tradition of Andrew's mission work, based apparently upon his interpretation of the Acts of Andrew and Matthias. "Andrew preached to the Iberians, Sauromatians, Taurians, and Scythians and to every region and city, on the Black Sea, both north and south." [2] Eventually, Andrew goes off to die, according to an unoriginal handling of Pseudo-Dorotheos and some version of the Acts of Andrew (probably *Epiphanios* or the *Laudatio*) [3].

The tenth century flowered with hagiography, most of it anonymous, some rather amusing. One of the more interesting is the Baptism of the Theotokos and the Holy Apostles, from which we learn that its author "inquired diligently and found in St. Sophronios' Commentaries, among others, these to be most worthy of memory. Only St. Peter was baptized by the Lord with His own hands, Andrew then by Peter, and James and John by Andrew. John baptized the rest of the Apostles." In a variant text, "Peter baptized Andrew and the sons of Zebedee, and Andrew and the sons of Zebedee the rest of the Apostles and the Seventy (Disciples)." [4]

After such wild legends, it is interesting to come to a hagiographer who makes his sources simpler and less improbable. Pseudo-Hippolytos, in his list of the Twelve and the Seventy, harks back to a hint found in Peter Chrysologus of Ravenna, who also placed the crucified Andrew on a tree. "Andrew, having preached to the Scythians and

---

[1] See 3, p. 19.
[2] *Oration* 4 *in Praise of St. Andrew*, PG 120, p. 64. Cf. Lipsius, *Ap.* I, pp. 182, 569 f, 608 f.
[3] *Ibid.*, pp. 75-80. Cf. Lipsius, *Ap.*, I, 569 f and 608 f.
[4] Schermann, *Vitae*, pp. 160-2.

the Thracians, was crucified in Patrae of Achaia upon an olive tree in an upright position and was buried there." [1] Stachys is called bishop of Byzantium and Philologos bishop of Sinope, but without any mention of Andrew!

Pseudo-Symeon Logothetēs ends the long list of pseudepigraphs in the Greek tradition. His story is really only a repetition of Pseudo-Epiphanios, whom, however, he corrects. Aegeates is no longer king (*basileús*) but ruler (*hēgemōn*). Andrew is again credited with the ordination of Stachys as bishop of Byzantium and Philologos as bishop of Sinope. [2]

The tenth century led to the crystalization of the Synaxaria and Menologia of the Greek Church. At least three variant forms are still in use; I shall quote only the longer form. "Andrew the First-Called and brother of Peter preached Christ along the whole coast of Bythinia, Pontus, and Armenia; and having passed through Pontus and Byzantium, he went as far as Greece. Crucified in Patrae of Achaia by Aegeates, he died." [3]

Certain mixed texts have also survived from this period in several manuscripts. One mixture is between Hippolytos and Dorotheos and places Andrew again in "great Sevastopol, where is the castle Psaros (*sic*) and the river Phasis, where the Ethiopians dwell inside."(!) [4] Another mixture, this time between the former mixture and Epiphanios, omits the inner- or inside- dwelling Ethiopians and simply send Andrew to Scythia again. [5]

The Greeks wished to know more about the ancestry of the Apostles. Rather unimaginatively, they said "Peter and Andrew, brothers, were from a father Johannes and a mother Johanna, fishermen by trade, from the village of Bethsaida." [6] The Ethiopian Church has preserved a more romantic text attributing each of the Apostles to a different tribe, yet leaving Peter and Andrew be brothers. According to Budge's translation, "The father of SIMON, who was surnamed PETER, and of ANDREW his brother, was of the house of RÔBÊL (REUBEN), and his mother's mother was of the house of SIMON (SIMEON); SIMON PETER's mother loved him greatly, and she named

---

[1] *Ibid.*, pp. 164, 168, 169.
[2] *Ibid.*, pp. 177, 180, 182, 185.
[3] *Ibid.*, p. 186, 1. 10 ff.
[4] *Ibid.*, p. 198, 1. 19 ff.
[5] *Ibid.*, p. 201.
[6] *Ibid.*, p. 203.

him SIMON after her father's family, and because ANDREW's father loved him greatly he counted him among the family of his father REUBEN." [1]

The Byzantine poetry concerning Andrew is plainly for memorization, rather than beauty. Johannes Euchaitensis' verses resemble most strongly those of Venantius Fortunatus, "Patraean men crucified likewise Andrew". [2] An anonymous poet, thinking probably of Theodoret's homily quoted above, in a homily by Pseudo-Chrysostomos sings that "Andrew corrected (diorthoō) the wise men of Greece." [3]

The Syriac texts are completely dependent on the Greek. Contemporaries may vary, however, in the use of texts which they had taken as a basis for their own chronicle. For example, Dionysius bar-Salibi (died 1171) uses an older source based on the Andrew-Matthias legend. I quote Chabot's French version and note: "André prêcha dans le pays de Beit-Kalbîn et sur tout le littoral; plus tard les Kalbê lui coupèrent les membres en morceaux. (Beit-Kalbîn = maison des chiens, on interprète généralement cette locution comme désignant la région des kynokéfaloi = Ethiopie.)" [4]

Yet his contemporary, Michael the Syrian (died 1199), uses the Epiphanian forgery as his basis, as do his successors. Again I quote Chabot's version "André precha a Nicée, a Nicomedie en Scythie y en Achaie, le premier il siégea a Constantinople et il y mourut." [5] The famous Bar-Hebraeus (died 1286) and the earlier chronicle-writer Solomon of Basrah (died c. 1222) simply repeat the Epiphanian version. [6]

Pseudo-Epiphanios and Pseudo-Dorotheos, therefore, are the most important of the later Greek and Syrian compilers of lists of the apostles. They alone add original, or unoriginal, material to what we have learned from the earlier fathers. It is to be noted that they emphasize the Andrew-Matthias tradition (which we have found as

---

[1] Budge, Ernest Alfred Wallis, *The Contendings of the Apostles*, vol. II, English text, p. 40 of 2nd ed. 1935; vol. I, Ethiopic text, p. 49 of 1st edition, 1899.

[2] Schermann, *Vitae*, p. 206, 1. 5.

[3] *Ibid.*, p. 206, 1. 5.

[4] Chabot, J. B., *Chronique de Michel le Syrien*, Paris, 1899, vol. I, fascicle 2, pp. 147 ff and note 1.

[5] *Ibid.*, p. 146.

[6] Bar-Ebrâjâ, *Chronicum Ecclesiaticum*, edidit Johannes Baptista Abbeloos et Thomas Joseph Lamy, Louvain, 1872, vol. I, p. 31 ff. Salomon of Basra, Book of the Bee, edited by E. A. W. Budge, in *Anecdota Oxoniensis, Semitic Series*, Oxford, 1886, vol. I, part II, p. 103 of English translation.

early as Origen) in their placing Andrew in Scythia. Both introduce
Stachys and Philologos as disciples of Andrew, who ordains them as
first bishops of Byzantium and Sinope, respectively. Pseudo-Dorotheos
is, however, completely original in his Zeuxippos story, altho it is
important to note that the Docetic concept of no real crucifixion for
Jesus is also present in his text. Photios simply re-introduces the
concept of a Leucios being the author of certain Acts of Andrew,
while the Greek and Ethiopian stories of the genealogies and baptism
of the apostles are clearly late Christian midrashīm.

A thorough search of the later literature, then, simply accomplished
the following:

1) In looking for signs of the original Acts of Andrew, one finds
   rather an increasing emphasis on the Andrew-Matthias legend of
   the visit to the City of the Cannibals (i.e., Scythia),
2) while, at the same time, less and less use is made of the Acts
   dealing with Greece and the Apostle's death at Patrae.
3) Byzantine desire to raise Constantinople to equality with Rome
   results in the Pseudo-Epiphanian and Pseudo-Dorothean forgeries.
4) Independently, a midrashic tendency leads to the formation of the
   genealogies and baptismal accounts.

CHAPTER SIX

DATE AND ORIGIN OF THE ORIGINAL ACTS OF ANDREW

Abbreviations used in this section for the various documents and Acts of Andrew (either alone or with other Apostles) are:

1) AA = The Acts of Andrew concerning *only* that Apostle as based on the following sources:

    I) E = Epiphanios (PG 120, pp. 215-260)

    II) NDP = Nicetas David Paphlogo (PG 105, pp. 53-80)

    III) Ep. = the Latin text of the Epistle of the presbyters and Deacons of Achaia's Churches (Bonnet, *Acta*, pp. 1-37)

    IV) Ep. Gr. = the longer Greek version of the above (ibid.)

    V) V = Vatican MS Greek 808 (ibid., pp. 38-45)

    VI) Mart. I = Martyrium (ibid., pp. 46-57)

    VII) Mart. II = Martyrium (ibid., pp. 58-64)

    VIII) L = Laudatio (Bonnet, *Suppl.*, pp. 3-44)

    IX) N = Narratio (ibid., pp. 46-64)

    X) P = Passio (ibid., pp. 66-70)

    XI) Gregory = Gregory of Tours' Book of St. Andrew's Miracles (edited by Bonnet, in *Monumenta Germaniae Historica, Scriptores Rerarum Merovingicarum*, Vol. I, pp. 821-47)

2) AM = Acts of Andrew and Matthias, (Bonnet, *Acta*, pp. 65-116)

3) PA = Acts of Peter and Andrew (ibid., pp. 117-127)

4) APh = Preaching of Andrew and Philemon (Budge, *Contendings*, Vol. II, 137-153 and pp. 307-334; Lewis, *Mythological Acts*, pp. 1-10)

5) ABa = Preaching of Andrew and Bartholomew (Budge, pp. 154-180; Lewis, pp. 11-25)

6) MAS = Martyrdom of Andrew in Scythia (Budge, pp. 181-185; Lewis, pp. 26-29)

Lipsius[1] developed a threefold analysis of the sources which placed the AA in the fourth of fifth centuries:

1) a catholic tradition concerning the Mission to the Scythians and their neighbors, which was at least before Origen (died c. 254);

---

[1] Lipsius, *Ap.* ,I, p. 598 ff.

24

2) a Gnostic (in its oldest form) tradition based on the AM and PA, which deal with the activity in Colchis on the Black Sea and the Ethiopians in the Land of the Cannibals.
3) and a late catholic tradition of the fourth century concerning the crucifixion in Patrae at the hands of the falsely labeled "King" Aegeas (or Aegeates).

Concerning the first viewpoint, there can be no doubt. The activity of the Apostle Andrew in Scythia, as has been shown above, was universally accepted in East and West, and indeed, even before any real mention of the Achaian Mission. Flamion [1], however, has shown clearly that the AM and PA are parts of the Greco-Egyptian cycle which was entirely of miracles and non-dogmatic revelations and which had no other purpose. More recent investigations, however, show that the AA deal in its earliest form with the Achaian Mission and the Passion of the Apostle in Patrae and, moreover, that the theological viewpoint was Gnostic-Docetic and not in any way catholic. Most important, the recovery of the Acts of Paul by Dr. Carl Schmidt, makes the dating of the whole cycle of early apocryphal acts in the second century. His arguments may be summarized as follows.

Tertullian's references to the Acts of Paul remain, as before, the *terminus ad quem* for those Acts. Taking into consideration Hippolytos' Commentary on Daniel, we must date the citation both by Tertullian and Hippolytos as not later than 203. [2] The Acts of Paul, then, were composed in the decade 190-200, at the very latest. However, the Acts of Paul are later than the Acts of Peter which must therefore be from the previous decade (or earlier), viz., 180-190. [3] Now Gregory definitely mentions the revelation to Andrew which predicts his death by crucifixion. "On the next night (Andrew) saw a vision, which he related:'... There stood by me my beloved brothers Peter and John; and John reached his hand to Peter and raised him to the top of the mountain, and turned to me and asked me to go up after Peter, saying: 'Andrew, you are to drink Peter's cup.' " [4]

---

[1] Flamion, J., *Les Actes Apocryphes de l'Apôtre André*, Louvain, 1911, pp. 301-309. Quispel, G., "An Unknown Fragment of the Acts of Andrew", *Vigiliae Christianae*, X, p. 144.

[2] Schmidt, Carl, *Praxeis Paulou, Acta Pauli, nach dem Papyrus der Hamburger Staats- und Universitätsbibliothek*, Hamburg, 1936, p. 127 f, see especially note 1. Quispel, p. 145.

[3] *Ibid.*, p. 130.

[4] Gregory of Tours, *Book of St. Andrew's Miracles*, section 20. Latin text edited by Maximilian Bonnet, *Monumenta Germaniae Historica, Scriptores Rerarum Mero-*

If, the dating of Peter (at the latest) is to be accepted as 180-190, then, it follows that the Acts of Andrew (whose definitely Gnostic origin speaks for an early date) were somewhat later, perhaps 190-200. However, the high point of Gnosticism is generally believed to be earlier. Moreover, the AM legend was already known to Origen. Lipsius' [1] thesis that the dogmatic works preceded the miracle-fables would imply, then, that time should be allowed for a sequence something as follows. First, the Gnostic AA, of which probably something was known, served as a scanty basis for the AM. Second, the AM legend had to have time to spread somewhat in order to have it come to Origen's attention. Origen, who would catagorically reject (if not ignore) the AA, would use the AM instead for his tradition of Andrew.

Hennecke and Schimmelpfeng have pointed out the closest connection between the Acts of John and the AA. [2] The above citation from Gregory confirms a literary dependence on this very early apocryphon (about 150)? I, therefore, suggest that the AA were an excessively lengthy composition in defense of Gnostic theology, which were composed in the last quarter of the second century. Because of its great length, the book was considerably ignored, probably even in Gnostic circles, and for that reason, AA is not cited by Tertullian or Hippolytos. Dr. Quispel of the University at Utrecht suggests even an earlier date (in the private interview mentioned below). [3]

A newly discovered Coptic fragment of the AA, presently in Dr. Quispel's possession, confirms the definitely Gnostic character, the very great length, and the probability of an early date. In a private interview, Dr. Quispel *generously* related the high points of his fragment. The copy dates from the fourth century and is on the reverse of a monkish story of the Patriarch Joseph. The Coptic is clearly a translation of the Greek, many of the words being left untranslated as is usually the case in Coptic translations.

Andrew comes to an unnamed city. His preaching created an uproar.

---

vingicarum, Gregorius Turonenisis, II, p. 837. Cf. James, *op. cit.*, p. 344; Flamion, *op. cit.*, p. 260; Hennecke, II, p. 547; Lipsius, *Ap.*, I, p. 559 f. Quispel, *op. cit.*, pp. 144 f, gives an other example.

[1] Lipsius, *Ap.*, I, p. 1.
[2] Hennecke, II, pp. 551-556.
[3] Dr. Quispel has since published his concepts. See footnotes and bibliography. Note his caution on p. 148 of his text.

A virgin, who is impressed by the Apostle's preaching, barely manages to defend herself against the wicked attempts at seduction of a magician. Andrew praises the saved virgin and exhalts the state of virginity. The brother of the virgin, himself a soldier, is sent to arrest Andrew. His gratitude to the Apostle on behalf of his sister is such that he takes off his uniform and deserts on the spot.

The incident is nowhere found in Gregory, either because it was already censored out of the Latin text in Gregory's possession or because the loyal Gregory, who would never have done anything to encourage desertion among his king's soldiers, himself cut the incident out. The fact that a new story can be found concerning Andrew from the AA confirms James' thesis that the AA must have originally been an extremely long book. [1]

Theologic peculiarities of the fragment are three:

1) that a soldier's nature (*phýsis*) rejects Christ, implying a predestination based on the nature of the individual's soul and exemplified in his profession or habits;
2) that God sends a *paralémptōr* who takes away the souls of the saints. This hapax legomenon occurs no place else in Greek literature, but the context makes it clear that it is a late nomen agentis from *paralambánō*, I take possession of, take away.
3) and that frequent references to God's Abode as the Palace (*palátion*) occur, e.g., the saints speak the "language of the Palace", or "the King has prepared for you a Palace."

This type of Gnostic theology is also found in V. "1 . . . about you is there only laziness? Have you not yet convinced yourselves that you are not yet bearing His goodness? We must be reverent, we must be joyful within ourselves in the rich fellowship which comes from Him. We must say to ourselves: Blessed is our race (*génos*)! Who has loved us? Blessed is our condition! Who has given us mercy? We are not of those thrown to the ground — we have been recognized by such a Greatness! We are not children of time, afterwards to be dissolved by time; neither are we products of motion, by which we are to be destroyed; nor are we by origin of birth, ending again in the same." [2] Again, in a speech to Maximilla, the unwilling wife of his future executioner Aegeates, Andrew clearly set forth the Gnos-

---

[1] James, *op. cit.*, p. 337.
[2] Bonnet, *Acta* "Ex Actis", p. 38, section 1. Cf. notes of Hennecke and Schimmelpfeng, Hennecke II, p. 551 f. Quispel, *op. cit.*, p. 142.

tic theology in undebatable terms." 6. Well-spoken! O nature (*phýsis*) being saved...! I recognize you who are more powerful than the merely apparent (*dokéō* participle) things which have overpowered you, who are more beautiful than the things throwing down into foulness, bringing you into captivity. Human (*ánthrope*) seeing all these things in himself: that you are immaterial (*á-ylos*), holy, light, a kinsman of the Unborn One, thoughtful, heavenly, transparent, clean above flesh and the world, above rulers and authorities—for, being above these, understanding yourself in your condition, and receiving the thought (*noûs*) by which you excell—see your own person in your own being, burst your chains, I tell you, not only the chains of birth but also of the above-birth (*tà hypèr génesin*). " [1]

This last selection of the Gnostic teaching of the AA, for we can hardly call it anything else, in view of its rejection of the material and of the born, is in the Aegeates story. Lipsius' thesis that the AM and PA were gnostic is, as Flamion showed, incorrect; Flamion's thesis that the AA were non-Gnostic, however, is equally incorrect. The original AA were the Gnostic-Manichaean books. Blatt's publication of the Latin versions [2] of the AM confirms the text of the better known Greek, Ethiopic, and Arabic versions which are quite non-dogmatic.

We must, then, consider a twofold tradition:

1) a Gnostic Acts of Andrew, of very great length, which dealt specifically with Andrew's adventures in Asia Minor and Greece, but which may have, at one time or another, contained a Scythian adventure.
2) a non-Gnostic, indeed, non-dogmatic, tradition which, perhaps borrowing a phase from the original AA, was developed into the Scythian-Cannibal legend of the AM and its successors.

The AA's possible reference to a cannibal adventure need have had no reference to a specific place. The Greek text of AM have no reference to Scythia whatever, while the Latin, Arabic, and Ethiopian legends identify Andrew's adventures in Scythia. The latter versions

---

[1] *Ibid.*, section 6. Cf. Hennecke II, pp. 552 f and especially Liechtenhan, R., *Die Offenbarung in Gnosticismus*, Göttingen, 1901, pp. 93-96, and *Die pseudepigraphische Literatur der Gnostiker*, in *Zeitschrift für die neutestamentliche Wissenschaft*, 1902, III, p. 295. Quispel, *op. cit.*, p. 143 f.

[2] Blatt, Franz, *Die lateinische Bearbeitung der Acta Andreae et Matthias apud anthropophagos*, Beiheft 12 zum *Zeitschrift für die neutestamentliche Wissenschaft*, 1930, p. 6. Cf. Quispel, *op. cit.*, p. 142 bottom note.

and Origen, too, were thinking undoubtedly of the cannibals mentioned in Herodotos. [1]

Flamion considered the AA to be the work of an Encratite who
probably lived in Patrae of Achaia, the scene of the martyrdom. [2]
Flatly, and without offering any arguments, he rejected the thesis of a
Gnostic origin, [3] such as Lipsius [4] and Liechtenhahn [5] saw. The latters'
theses have already been defended above. Flamion's concept that the
AA were composed at Patrae rests upon two points:

1) The names of all the principals except Maximilla, of course, —
   including the proconsuls, Lesbios and Aegeates — are Greek.
   That a person living in the Roman Empire should give everyone,
   even Romans, Greek names shows clearly that "history" was
   not the purpose of the AA and the author's thinking geographically
   was thoroughly provincial Greek.
2) There are three missions to Achaia, whose proconsul at Patrae
   is a central figure. No other region so dominates the story, altho
   the travelling missions to Asia Minor and Thrace-Macedonia are
   important enough.
       In defense of a generally Eastern origin, I would add that
3) besides the Greek language and scene, the Gnostic theology
   argues more than the Encratitic for an Eastern origin.

Flamion, by dating the AA in the third century and by his denial
of the Gnostic origin, thought these two points favored Achaia in
particular. However, the reverse is rather the case, but his first two
arguments stand. These points, however, do suggest that the AA
arose in Christian Gnostic circles, possibly in Achaia, certainly in
Greece or Asia Minor. That the Acts of Peter and those of John,
attributed to Anatolian authorship, were the predecessors of AA would
indicate origin from this general region.

---

[1] PW, article, "andróphagoi".
[2] Flamion, *op. cit.*, pp. 266-8. Quispel protests against this thesis and that
of my note 3, below, *op. cit.*, p. 143, note 17.
[3] *Ibid.*, p. 152, note 6. "Nous ne comprenons pas la prétention de Liechtenhan."
Cf. Quispel's protest above.
[4] Lipsius, *Ap.*, I, p. 598 ff.
[5] Liechtenhan, see note 2, p. 27.

CHAPTER SEVEN

RECONSTRUCTION OF THE ACTS OF ANDREW

Four scholars, Pick [1], Hennecke [2], Flamion [3], and James [4] have attempted reconstructions of the Acts of Andrew. The first two, Pick and Hennecke, however, really attempted only a reconstruction of the Passion of Andrew as it would have been found in the AA. Both made the error of omitting the Gregorian text. Flamion went farther and made a detailed analysis of the sources and suggested in detail which belonged to the AA and which to later hands. His reconstruction included Gregory; because Flamion did not actually write a reconstructed text, James in his *Apocryphal New Testament* did so, combing Flamion's suggestions with the second edition of Hennecke. James' reconstructed and translated text, as it stands, is nearly complete, lacking only the Utrecht fragment.

My own suggestion is essentially the same. One takes as the basis for the beginning of Andrew's missionary career Gregory, but omitting the two sections which merely repeat the AM legends. Andrew is in Achaia throughout the first part of the story (sections 3-4) and goes to Sinope. It is here in section 5 I suggest that one may insert the Utrecht fragment, for the mission in Sinope is very shortly treated and alone has no incident of persecution such as mentioned in the Utrecht fragment. It also deals with a chastity problem, in which a mother attempts incest with her son. Sections 6 to 10 cover a mission to Macedonia. In contradiction to the Dorothean forgery, Andrew does go to Byzantium but meets no Zeuxippos. Section 11, as James has already suggested, should be corrected in the light of the Epistle of Titus incident. In Gregory, Andrew stops two cousins from marrying, while, in the apocryphal Epistle, he stops a marriage between two unrelated families.

Sections 12 to 19 relate a number of miracles and persecutions in

---

[6] Pick, Bernhard, *The Apocryphal Acts of Paul, Peter, John, Andrew, and Thomas,* Chicago and London, 1909, pp. 215 on. Very incomplete.

[2] Hennecke, I, pp. 464-473; II, pp. 549-561. Most learned, the basis of the two following.

[3] Flamion, *op. cit.*, pp. 89-263 is more a criticism as a reconstruction. Against Flamion and James, see Quispel, *op. cit.*, p. 148 cf. his pp. 137 ff.

[4] James, *op. cit.*, pp. 337-363. The most complete.

Thessalonica and in Philippi of Macedonia. Section 20 contains the already quoted revelation which tells Andrew that like Peter he is to be crucified. James' suggestion that Jesus should be read instead of John is a reasonable conjecture; but, since John was always a favorite of the Gnostic school and because of the close connection of the AA with the Acts of John, I see no reason to change the text. Sections 21 to 29 tell of Andrew's second mission to Achaia, in much fuller detail than in Laudatio 27-30. Gregory's section 30-35 again find a correspondence in Laudatio but, since this time Laudatio gives a fuller account in its sections 38 to 44 it should be followed. In section 35 of Gregory, Andrew is finally thrown into prison by the angry Aegeates, at which time the whole of two quotations of Evodius should be inserted. Gregory sections 36 to 38 should be entirely omitted since the full Passion story of Andrew can be reconstructed from other documents.

First comes the V account with its long sermons. N 22 and Mart. II, 1 tell how Stratokles, Aegeates' brother, attempts to stop the execution. N 24 and Mart. II, 3 relate Aegeates' orders to ignore his brother, who is consoled by Andrew. N 26 brings Andrew to his place of execution by the shore, while L 46, Mart I, 14 and Ep. Gr. 10 give Andrew's speech of welcome to his cross. N 28 tells how Andrew was finally placed on the cross and spoke to the multitude on the evil of idolatry. All the sources, Ep. Gr, N, Mart II, and P join in describing the anger of the people against Aegeates, while Andrew urges the crowd to permit his execution. Aegeates finally approaches the cross to remove Andrew, who refuses. P adds that Andrew was surrounded by a great glory in the moment of his death, which echoes yet in the *Martyrologium Romanum*. It is, however, omitted by N, which adds that Maximilla, Aegeates' wife, abandoned the proconsul and that his brother, Stratokles refused the wealth he inherited after the death of Aegeates.

Such a reconstruction will give, however, only an idea of the order of events; the true theology of the Acts of Andrew can be found only in the Utrecht and Vatican fragments and, to a lesser extent, in Narratio.

CHAPTER EIGHT

ACTS OF ANDREW AND MATTHIAS

Altho no connection between the AA and the AM can be shown, except that Gregory combined the two books, it is not unreasonable to assume that the earlier, Gnostic AA may have contained an incident which was expanded into the AM. The fabulous AM were, as shown above, probably composed after the AA (after 190) and before 254, the death of Origen. Complete copies survive not only in the original Greek, but also in Ethiopic [1], Arabic [2], Syriac [3], and Latin [4] which has a daughter version in Anglo-Saxon [5]. In spite of minor variants, all the versions show none of the Gnostic tendencies of the AA. Rather, this is the first of the miracle romances, which were manufactured in such large quantities in Greece and especially in Egypt. The frequent references to Scythia in Origen and his successors surely refer to the AM. The newly published Latin versions specifically introduce the name of the land as Scythia and of the city as Myrmidona or Mermedonia, which Gutschmid has identified with Myrmēkiōn, a city in the Taurian Cheronese (Crimea). [6] Behind the learned Origen's thinking was probably Herodotos' references to the *andróphagoi* in Scythia. [7] The Syriac texts identify the city of the Cannibals (*anthropóphagoi*) with a certain 'Irqâ [8]; but this should be regarded as an isolated Syriac interpretation.

In the present form, the AM has no probable relationship to the AA, except in the beginning of the AM. Here one finds the very

---

[1] Budge, *op. cit.*, vol. I, pp. 225-246 and 307-335; vol. II, pp. 223-240 and 307-334. Quispel, *op. cit.*, p. 136, note 4 has cited Budge's p. 150 as containing a tradition about Andrew.

[2] Lewis, Agnes Smith, *Horae Semiticae* III, *Acta Mythologica Apostolorum*, London, 1904, fol. 129a (end) to fol. 139b of vol. I, Arabic text; English, vol. II, pp. 126-136.

[3] Wright, William, *Apocryphal Acts of the Apostles*, London, 1871, vol. I, Syriac text, pp. 102-126; vol. II, English version, pp. 93-115.

[4] Blatt, *op. cit.*

[5] Grimm, Jakob, *Andreas und Elene*, Kassel, 1841.

[6] Von Gutschmid, Alfred, *Kleine Schriften*, Leipzig, 1890; vol. II, p. 383 = "Die Königsnamen in den apokryphen Apostelgeschichten," *Rheinisches Museum für Philologie*, N.F., vol. XIX, 1864, p. 394.

[7] See footnote 1, p. 29.

[8] Wright, *op. cit.*, vol. I, p. 126; vol. II, p. 115.

interesting theory that the Apostles on Pentecost drew lots in order to decide their mission fields. This is an item mentioned frequently in the lists of the Apostles cited above. In some texts, the relatively unknown Apostle Matthias is replaced by the more famous Disciple, Apostle, and Evangelist Matthew. This is a confusion similar to false identification of Simon Barjona with the familiar Simon Peter, which was discussed in the first chapter.

The confused incident found in sections 12 to 15 in the Greek text of the AM demonstrates two facts about its origin. First, because this section is abbreviated or drastically changed in the Syriac and Arabic version, it shows, by the law of the *lectio difficilior*, that the original language of the AM is Greek. This is also shown in Wright's Syriac text which gives mistranslations only possible from Greek into Syriac and not the reverse. Second, this section begins with a visit to a *pagan* temple, but the argument is between the *Jewish* High Priests and Jesus. The Greek is of a different type, e.g., AM usually uses *pneuma*, but this section uses *pnoe*. The style and vocabulary is like the AA and not at all like the rest of AM. This, too, may have formed a part of AA. Gregory and Gregory's successor, Pseudo-Abdias, join with the Greek fathers in combining the two legends, always putting AM at the beginning. [1]

---

[1] Gregory in Bonnet's text in MGH, pp. 837 f. Abdias in Fabricius, Johannes Albert, *Codex Apocryphus Novi Testamenti*, Hamburg, 1743, vol. II, pp. 457 ff. Bonnet, *Sup.*, Laudatio, p. 25, section 29; Narratio, pp. 48-50, sections 4-7.

CHAPTER NINE

VARIATIONS OF THE ACTS OF ANDREW
AND MATTHIAS

The AM, as has been mentioned, left more than the above translated Greek text as a literary remain. In the Latin versions, the silence of the Greek original on the location of the City of the Cannibals was removed and the scene definately located at Mymēkiōn in the Crimea. [1]

The Syriac version, in an obviously added conclusion, said the Cannibals were in 'Irqâ. [2] It also re-identified the companion-saint of Andrew as Matthew. The Arabic texts make no attempt at identification of the City of the Cannibals, but do give an entirely new version of Andrew's martyrdom. [3] This story is also found in the Ethiopic cycle of legends. [4] Lipsius considered the cycle of the Scythian martyrdom to be the originally Gnostic AA [5]; but as demonstrated above, this seems most unlikely.

The Arabic-Ethiopic Martyrdom of Andrew in Scythia (MAS) was originally written in Coptic, altho the Coptic original is no longer extant. The story is very short and may be briefly (by combining Budge's and Lewis' translations) [6] told: Andrew goes to the cities of Aknîs (Ethiopic Askâtyâ, i.e., Scythia) and Argyânôs (i.e., Garanius) and Safras (Ethiopic Suqes, i.e., Axis). In the last he preaches. Messengers are sent to persuade him to leave, but are converted by Andrew. The evil rulers threaten to burn Andrew alive, but are burned by heavenly fire instead. Some evil men still survive and throw Andrew in prison. He prays for their destruction, but the Lord tells Andrew that his work is finished. The next day the people take Andrew out to be crucified. They threw stones at him until he died.

As the story stands, it is completely lacking in any purpose whatever except that of killing Andrew off to finish the cycle. It is interesting, however, to note that the oldest tradition of Andrew's mission, the

---

[1] Blatt, *op. cit.*, p. 6. cf. my footnote 6, p. 32.
[2] Wright, *op. cit.*, vol. I, p. 126; vol. II, p. 115.
[3] Lewis, *op. cit.*, vol. I, fol. 42a-44b; vol. II, pp. 26-29.
[4] Budge, *op. cit.*, vol. I, pp. 184-188; vol. II, pp. 181-185.
[5] Lipsius, *Ap.*, p. 598 f.
[6] Budge, *op. cit.*, vol. II, pp. 181-185; Lewis; *op. cit.*, vol. II, pp. 26-29.

one to Scythia, is here combined with a martyrdom story. One rather has the impression that the Scythian mission became isolated from the AM in Egypt, because Scythia is not named in the Egyptian AM text. Therefore, a later hagiographer had to fill in the gap and wrote this very short episode to complete the cycle.

Eventually, it was inevitable that someone should combine the work of the two brothers, Peter and Andrew, into a separate "Acts of Peter and Andrew." This survives in Greek and Slavonic [1]; but in the Ethiopic cycle is told of Peter and Thaddaeus, not Andrew [2]. The Ethiopic text is considerably abridged from the Greek original, while the colophon interestingly enough attributed the work to our old friends, Sophronios and Dorotheos. No use is made of either Pseudo-Dorotheos or of Pseudo-Sophronios anywhere in the Egyptian-Ethiopic cycle, yet their names are listed among the authors. Apparently, there was still some life in the ecclesiastic contacts between Byzantium and Ethiopia even after the ninth century, but no more than that can be stated as an explanation of this surprising attribution of authorship.

The PA should be dated about the second half of the third century, roughly contemporanaeous with the beginning of monasticism. The legend is one of the earliest and most popular of the defenses of the monastic movement, incorporating, as it does, the wonder of miracles, the holiness of poverty, and purity of the chaste life. The PA still echoes not only the AM (whose sequel it is) but also the old AA. Upon the arrival of the Apostles at the City of the Barbarians, the devil exclaims "Woe to us, these are of the twelve Galilaeans who practise magic on men, for they separate men from their wives and women from their husbands." AA 's teaching that marriage was evil was still quoted even after the AA was being condemned and lost. The devil suggested putting a wanton woman in the gateway to stop the Apostles. Andrew (reminiscent of AM) suggested that he pray, Michael coming to lift the prostitute up in the air until the Apostles would safely enter the city. The rich Onesiphorus forces the Apostles to make a camel go thru the eye of a needle several times and is converted, giving his money to the poor. The wanton woman in the air is also converted and sets up a nunnery.

PA introduces not only monasticism in a recognizable form to the

---

[1] Greek in Bonnet, *Acta*, pp. 117-127. Slavonic in Bonwetsch, *Zeitschrift für Kirchengeschichte*, V. 1882, p. 506 on, cited by Bonnet.

[2] Budge, *op. cit.*, vol. I, pp. 296-306; vol. II, pp. 296-305.

Andrew cycle, but also brings Alexander and Rufus from Mark 15 : 21 to assist the Apostles. This *motif* is carried out also in the Preaching of Andrew and Philemon (APh), which is the immediate sequel to the Peter and Andrew story. According to the APh, Andrew had released Rufus and Alexander from his following, so that they might follow Matthias to the Cannibal City. The APh, however lacking in the anti-sexual, the love of poverty, or the love of dogma which characterized the earlier Acts about Andrew, does include a slightly greater regard to some historic possibility. The governor of Lydda (Acts 9 : 32-43) has the believable Roman name of Rufus and can be afraid of the Emperor. Both the surviving Arabic text and its Ethiopic version attribute the events to the land of the Kurds and the city of Lydda. Only the latter is mentioned in the story, while the former place is referred to only in the beginning. I doubt if any story of Andrew sent him to the Kurds, but suggest that a copier of the original may have had the Scythians in mind. To a later age, the difference between Kurds and Scythians may not have been very distinct. The story in its present form is certainly of Egyptian origin, but apparently of a completely undogmatic type.

Lydda was already half converted by Peter (Acts 9 : 35); Andrew and Philemon were to accomplish the conversion of the rest of the city. Philemon sings so sweetly in the church that some pagan priests who came to kill the Christians are converted. While Andrew is personally baptising five thousand people, the devil causes a nobleman's son to be killed by the son of John (according to the Arabic, a sheikh; Ethiopic, a priest). The nobleman lets John go look for Andrew, while he holds John's son captive. Andrew sends Philemon, who is arrested by the governor, Rufus, at the instigation of the devil. Philemon's begging for mercy shows the complete lack of theologic thinking by the author. "O Governor Rufus! Do not torture me, for I am an infant, I have not sinned, and I do not deserve a condemnation." The soldiers weep because of the sweetness of his voice, but do not release him. Where in earlier Acts, sex is simply condemned, in the APh, we find a developed sense of humor. A sparrow offers to fly to Andrew on Philemon's behalf. Philemon says, "You are a fornicator, you will not hasten your return, for if you meet a hen of your kind, you will stop with her and will not hasten your return." A raven is refused because he returned not to Noah (Gen. 8 : 7); but a dove is sent.

Rufus, astonished, is converted. Satan causes his wife to kill

Rufus' children. Upon being informed, Rufus insists on staying with Philemon. Andrew comes and tells Philemon to resurrect the dead son of the nobleman and does so.

The boy tells of a visit to Gehenna, where a house was built for his father, who was to burn in it after his death. Jesus (not mentioned but identifiable because of his Lordship and his being in the form of a twelve year old boy) pardons the boy's father and orders the house in Gehenna destroyed and one built in Heaven. Rufus (who is now identified as the boy's father!) is converted on the spot. Rufus' wife is found holding a Negro in her hand, who identifies himself as the demon Māgānā (so the Arabic; Ethiopic Makâr) who was one of two hundred fallen angels. Andrew banishes him to Gehenna, heals Rufus' wife, and prepares for his next mission. Rufus becomes his disciple, assisting at the cure of a man possessed by demons, giving his wealth to the poor, and laughing at the Emperor's messengers who came to confiscate his wealth.

For all its simplicity and inconsistency, the APh is still an original story. Its sequel, however, the Preaching of Andrew and Bartholomew (ABa) is quite unoriginal, copying the Andrew and Matthias legend for the most part. Like the APh, the scene is probably Palestine, Mâctarân being the Magadán of Matthew 15 : 39 and Ghâryanûs being the Gadarēnoí of Mark 5 : 1.

In this last region, Bartholomew is preaching, when the Lord commands him to go to the Land of the Barbarians (cf. AM end and AP). Andrew, who is somewhere else, leaves with his disciples, Rufus and Alexander, to join Bartholomew. As in the AM, Jesus (unknown to the Apostle) magically transports them, first in a fish to Gadarēnoí where he meets Andrew in a boat. Jesus, still unknown, pretends to be a budding convert. The wife of the ruler of Macedonia is carried by the sea to them at Jesus' command and cured of her demon.

Jesus prays that they all be taken to the Land of the Barbarians, the Apostles grow wings and fly there, landing on a temple and finally recognizing Jesus, who blesses and leaves them. Gallio the Governor has the Apostles and the pagan priests contest each other. The Apostles make the idols fly to the top of the temple and confess that they are no gods. The devil incites the crowd to burn the Apostles. Three times they fail to kill by burning, once by sawing, and finally by stoning. The unconscious four, Andrew, Bartholomew, Rufus and Alexander are thrown out of the walls. Jesus sends an angel who *forces* a man with a dog's head to believe in the True God by surrounding Dog's Head with fire. The five now return to the city of the Barbarians, where Dog's Head, in order to save the Apostolic four, attacks and kills eleven lions and two tigers. The Lord surrounds the city with fire (as in AM) and the people, afraid of Dog's Head and of the fire, surrender and become Christians. Andrew kicks a statue which pours forth water for the baptisms. The reference to Dog's Head, who is supposed to be from Cannibal City, reminds one of the Syriac text of AM and Dionysius Bar-Salibi's reference to it, for they call the Cannibal City "House of the Dogs." [1]

The Acts of Peter and Andrew, of Andrew and Philemon, and of Andrew and Bartholomew, all possess the redeeming quality of little or no anti-Jewish feeling, whereas the AA and the AM are full of anti-Jewish remarks. Another Egyptian (this time surviving only in a Coptic fragment) story has Paul or Philemon accompany Andrew on his mission. The stories are quite anti-Jewish. The two fragments are in poor condition but a consistent tale can be reconstructed from the repetitious nature of the style.

In the first fragment, which James and Lipsius call the Acts of Andrew and Paul, Paul has already dived into the sea to visit Amente, the land of the dead. The captain of the ship accidentally cures his nearly blind mother with Paul's cloak. Andrew goes off to cure a twelve-year old boy at the request of his father; but the Jews will not let him in the city. The father is told not to bury his son until Andrew returns, for the lad dies in the meantime. Upon his return to the ship, the captain shows Andrew where Paul entered the water. Andrew's prayer and a cup of fresh water split the sea so that Paul returns with a piece of wood from Amente in his hand. Paul's description of the underworld shows us something of late Coptic theology. Judas Iscariot was almost alone in Amente, since the Ressurrected Jesus had rescued the other souls, except for some murderers, magicians, and throwers of little children into water! Judas is not punished for his betrayal of Jesus but for his worshipping Satan (after Jesus had once forgiven him!) and for his suicide. Satan thought he would always possess Judas, but Jesus had assured Judas of a better fate. Meanwhile Judas was to stay in Amente. [2]

---

[1] See note 4, p. 22.

[2] Guidi, Ignazio, *Gli Atti Apocrifi degli Apostoli nei Testi Copti, Arabi, ed Etiopi in Giornale della Società Asiatica Italiana*, II, 1888, pp. 45 f. Dulaurier, A., *Fragments des révélations apocryphes de S. Barthélemy*, Paris, 1835, p. 30 ff. Cf., James, *op. cit.*, pp. 472-474 and Lipsius, *Ap.*; IV, p. 95 f.

The Apostles, with Appolonius the captain, are still refused entrance by the Jews. They send a scarab (Greek *díkairon*, which the Coptic calls *díkaion*-righteous) to the dead boy's father. The people are angry because of the Jews and threaten to stone them. The governor intervenes and, as the Jews suggest, tells the Apostles to open the gates themselves, if God had sent them. Paul then hits the gates with his piece of wood from Amente and they disappear in the earth. About two leaves are lost here; apparently the Jews prepared a fraud about a dead man. Seemingly, too, the dead boy had been raised.

Before the dead man, the Apostles asked that he be untied. The Jews try to flee, but are stopped by soldiers until the "dead" man is free. He begs forgiveness and tells "everything that had happened." Andrew accuses the Jews of trickery. A mass conversion of about 27,000 Jews then takes place. A part of the same Coptic fragment tells of a woman who killed her child and fed it to her dog. She fled as the Apostles approach. Philemon (who appears in the Arabic-Ethiopic "Preaching") is consulted. The resulting prayer alludes to a miracle by Jesus on Mount Gebal "when, a great multitude being gathered, Thou didst command that all the scattered stones and grains of sand be gathered in one place." The child seems to have come together again and to live, for in the surviving fragments it laughs and weeps.

Altho probably of Greek origin (see the mistake or pun on *díkai-(r)on*), these two Coptic fragments have apparently no connection either with the Utrecht fragment of the AA, nor with the AM and its successors in the Egyptian cycle of legends. However, since the known literature concerning Andrew (much less concerning Andrew's fellow-Apostles) was so vast that it can be traced through a long genealogy, we need not be surprised at an extra story appearing from time to time.

CHAPTER TEN

THE GENEALOGY OF THE ANDREW LEGENDS

The development of the cycle of stories about the Apostles is in each case somewhat different. Nevertheless, most of the legends are dependent, one upon the other, to such an extent that a general rule can be postulated. Lipsius' dogma that, while the true facts of history may have preceeded the dogmatic story, certainly the Heils-geschichte with a doctrine preceeded the stories of miracles. A diagrammatic description of the development of the Andrew Legends follows. [1]

It will be noted that the forgeries of Pseudo-Epiphanios and Pseudo-Dorotheos find no reflexion in the West at all in the Middle Ages. When the *Martyrologium Romanum* was published about 1518, we find our first Western mention of Stachys as Bishop of Byzantium by

A. — BEGINNING AND THE EGYPTIAN CYCLE.

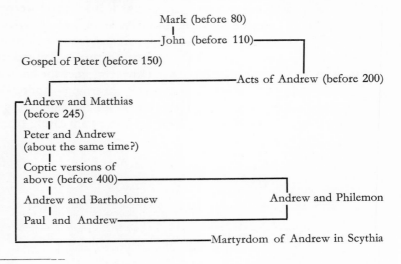

---

[1] Diagram A is based on Guidi, *op. cit.*, pp. 1 f. B and D based in part on Schermann, *Propheten*, p. 353, who attributes too much to Syriac tradition. C. is completely my own work. I agree with Diekamp's suggestion that the Laudatio is
based on Epiphanios. See Diekamp, F., *Hippolytos von Theben*, Münster, 1898, pp.
144 f as against Lipsius, *Ap.*, I, 574.

B. THE BYZANTINE LEGENDS

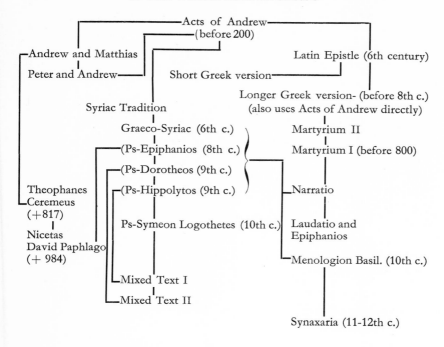

C. THE LATIN TRADITION

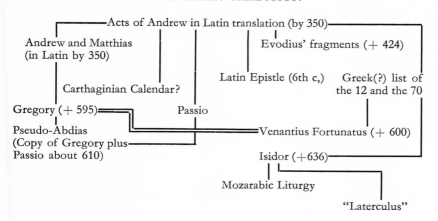

D. THE SYRIAC TRADITION

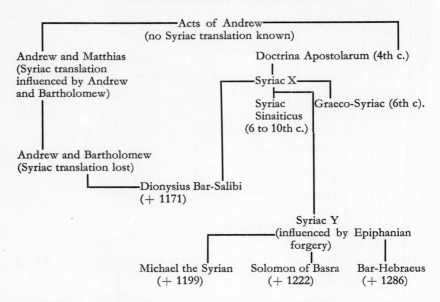

Andrew's ordination. At no earlier time is a reference to be found. The reference itself occurs in 31 October, the day of Stachys, not under the 30 November, the day of Andrew's martyrdom. The text of the *Martyrologium Romanum* is taken from the *Passio* (for 30 November). [1]

Similarly it finds no reflexion in the Egyptian cycle, except for the peculiar attribution of the cycle to Dorotheos in one Ethiopic manuscript. [2] The Egyptian cycle made no impression on the Latin or Greek stories, altho the reference to the Dog's Head seems to have impressed the Syrian Dionysius Bar-Salibi [3]. The Acts of Andrew and Matthias and the Martyrdom of Andrew (as originally found in the AA), however, greatly influenced all the literatures. Eventually, the Egyptian cycle threw out the Patrae martyrdom entirely with the Acts of Andrew; but the Utrecht fragment shows that the AA was popular among Coptic monks. Later Coptic theology preferred to invent its own cycle to keeping the AA, which must have been most verbose, if not too deep for the last of the Copts who had a copy.

The wholly anti-Gnostic West preserved the outline of the whole of the Gnostic AA in Gregory. Byzantium, except for the Epiphanian

---

[1] Bonnet, *Sup.*, p. 70 and *Acta*, pp. 33 f.
[2] Budge, *op. cit.*, Vol. I, p. 306 and vol. II, p. 306.
[3] Chabot, *op. cit.*, pp. 148 f. Cf. Lipsius, *Ap.*, p. 547.

forgery, contributed no cycle of legends to Andrew's fame, as did the Egyptians. Egypt, whose Monophysite Church was always friendlier to Gnosticism, abandoned after the fifth century the AA entirely, substituting the (probably already a century old) cycle of legends about the Apostles composed in Egypt but preserved in Arabic and Ethiopic. The irony of accidents which make up the survival of ancient literature through the Middle Ages is climaxed, as Hennecke pointed out, by the German use of Andrew in folklore. The originally anti-sexual, even anti-matrimonial, Andrew is in modern times the saint of women seeking men. [1]

---

[1] Hennecke II, pp. 561 f.

Dates have been taken from the above listed literature, except in cases of certain Fathers of the Church in which case Heussi, Latourette, and Walker have been followed.

CHAPTER ELEVEN

ANDREW IN CHRISTIAN ART.

As with the legends of Andrew, the artistic themes about him are Eastern products brought to the West. Because of the minor importance of Andrew as compared with Peter or Paul, and because the "Acts of Andrew" were so unpopular with Catholic bishops, artists left the First-Called pretty much alone until after the time of the Pseudo-Dorothean forgery.

John's picture of Andrew and Philip in the Feeding of the Five Thousand is the scene for the first representation of Andrew in Christian Art. It occurs in a fifth-century catacombe in Egypt. [1] The same theme occurs on at least one Italian sarcophagus before the end of the eight century. [2]

The Call of Andrew, again following the Gospel of John, was another theme imported into the West from the East. The sixth century mosaics of the church of San Apollinare Nuovo at Ravenna picture John the Baptist pointing Jesus out to Andrew. [3] Unexplained, or perhaps unexplainable, is the unusual head of Andrew which is found only in the frescos in Santa Maria Antiqua in Rome. [4] Although it dates from about 705, it differs from the standard which is to be found on a statue in Amalfi. The Amalfi statue is of the twelfth century, [5] and agrees with Durandus' description of our Apostle in 1551. "Saint Andrew was dark in his complexion, with a long beard, and of average stature. This therefore is said that it may be known how he ought to be painted in the church, for it is necessary to know this about each of the apostles and many other saints." [6] I should add

---

[1] Kaufmann, K. M., *Handbuch der Christlichen Archaeologie*, Paderborn, 1905, p. 387.

[2] Garricci, R., *Storia dell' Arte Cristiana nei Primi Otto Secoli della Chiesa*, Prato, 1872-1880, Plate 426.

[3] Wilpert, Joseph, *Die römischen Mosaiken und Malereien der kirchlichen Bauten vom 4. bis 13. Jahrhundert*, Freiburg, 1917, Tafel 97.

[4] *Ibid.*, Tafel 157.

[5] Rohault de Fleury, *Les Saints de la Messe*, Paris, 1883 f, t. X. plate 12.

[6] Durandus, Guillielmus, *Prodiron*, Lugduni, 1551, chapter VII, 38, 1 cited by Timmers, J. J. M., *Symboliek en Iconographie der Christelijke Kunst*, Roermond-Maaseck, 1947, p. 864. Cf. Johannes Malanus, *De Historia Sanctorum Imaginum et Picturarum*, Lovanii, 1771, (editio J. N. Pacquot), p. 384 f.

that Andrew is usually seen as an old man, often bald, with one or two books in his hands (a reference to the "Acts of Andrew" or to the Muratorian legend of his connection with the Gospel of John). Not infrequently, due to the influence of the fisherman tales of Mark and Matthew, Andrew is presented with fish, fishing net, rope, or ship in the background. [1] The fish, of course, is in itself an old Christian symbol. Among other values, the Greek word for fish, ichthys, was interpreted *Iesûs Christòs Theû Yiòs Sóter*, i.e., Jesus the Anointed, God's Son, Savior.

The theme of Andrew's crucifixion comes, obviously, not from the Gospels, but from the Apocryphal Acts of Andrew. The first series of crucifixions show not the famous X-shaped cross, but the familiar Latin cross used in Jesus' crucifixion. The oldest surviving representations of Andrew's crucifixion are Byzantine miniatures in ninth-century manuscripts. [2] It is interesting to note that it was about this time that the Epiphanian and Dorothean forgeries appeared. On both these miniatures, Andrew is nailed (as with the Johannine crucifixion of Jesus) but not tied (as is described in the Acts of Andrew). In the eleventh century bronze gate of St. Paul's at Rome, Andrew is also nailed, interestingly enough, to a Y-shaped cross. [3]

The oldest representation of Andrew's being tied to the cross occurs in a sacramentar at Pruem. [4] The famous X-shaped cross makes its appearance first on a troparium from Autun, which is of tenth century manufacture. [5] It should be remembered that before this all crosses of Andrew were Latin in form.

Also on a Latin cross again is our Apostle in the oldest representation, which shows others present at the crucifixion. In a sacramentar at Ivrea, made about 1000, Andrew is shown in the center on his cross, while to his left stands a military executioner who ties him to

---

[1] Cf. Roeder, Helen, *Saints and Their Attributes*, New York, 1955, Article, "Apostles". Droulers, Eugene, *Dictionnaire des Attributes Allégories, Emblèmes et Symboles*, Turnhout, n.d., p. 15. Husenbeth, F. C., *Emblems of the Saints*, Norwich, 1882, article "Andrew".

[2] One is in a codex of the Homilies of Gregory of Nazianus, plate 30 in Ormont's *Facsimilés des Miniatures des plus anciens Manuscripts grecs de la Bibliothèque Nationale*, Paris, 1902. The other is in a Greek Menologion of the Vatican Library and is mentioned by Karl Künstle, *Ikonographie der Heiligen*, Band II, Freiburg, 1926, pp. 59-61. This is a more modern re-write of Heinrich Detzel's *Christliche Ikonographie*, Freiburg, 1896, Band,II, pp. 132-135, de Fleury, *op. cit.*, plates 47 and 48.

[3] Husenbeth, *op. cit.*, article "Andrew". Cf. Cahier, Charles, *Charactéristiques des Saints dans l'Art populaire*, Paris, 1866, p. 286.

[4] De Fleury, *op. cit.*, plate 49.

[5] De Fleury, *op. cit.*, plate 8.

it. On the right a king (the unidentified Aegeates) sits with scepter in hand on his throne. [1] A more complete picture appears in a missal, from France, apparently. On the left the crowd is staring at Andrew, while on the right an angry judge sits on his chair. [2]

Since the Acts of Andrew were lost to the East, it is naturally the West which has preserved the only paintings of Andrew the missionary. In very similar glass paintings at Troyes and Auxerre one can see Andrew chasing away seven demons in the form of dogs. In the background is Nicaea. The paintings are from the thirteenth century. [3] The source is Gregory's censored abridgment of the Acts of Andrew.

Still later in Rome, Guido Reni and Domenchino used Pseudo-Abdias's *Apostolic History* (itself a combination of Gregory's book and the *Passio*) to paint a series on Andrew's crucifixion. Reni painted, in the Church of Saint Gregory on Mont Celia, Andrew worshipping the cross, with the walls of Patrae in the background. The Apostle is accompanied by soldiers, women, and children and falls to the ground as soon as he sees the cross. Domenchino in the Church of St. Andrea della Valle, also in Rome, shows John the Baptist pointing out Jesus to Andrew, Jesus calling Andrew, the executioners torturing Andrew, Andrew's worshipping the cross, and, finally, Andrew being carried to Heaven by angels. [4]

Andrew in art parallels the career of Andrew in literature. In both, at first, the Gospels are used. Later, the legendary sources replace the original Good News.

---

[1] Ebner, Adelbert, *Quellen und Forschungen zur Geschichte und Kunstgeschichte des römischen Missale*, Freiburg, 1896, pp. 60.

[2] *Ibid.*, p. 207.

[3] Mâle, Emile, *L'Art religieux du XIIIe Siècle en France*, Paris, 1898, p. 390.

[4] Künstle, *op. cit.*, p. 61, Detzel, *op. cit.*, p. 135.

CHAPTER TWELVE

GENERAL CONCLUSIONS

Andrew makes his appearance in history in the Gospel of Mark. That *no* reliable tradition existed about him in the ancient church is shown not only by the silence of the Acts of the Apostles but also by the fact that Luke and Matthew *omit* even Mark's impersonal references to Peter's brother. As early as John (certainly before 110), the historic Andrew has been replaced by the legendary Disciple-Apostle. Quite possibly, as Dr. Cullmann suggests, the Fourth Evangelist used Andrew as a sort of anti-Peter. It is certain that Pseudo-Epiphanios and Pseudo-Dorotheos did in the ninth century set up Andrew the First-Called of the Apostles against Peter the Prince of the Apostles, by imagining Andrew as founder of the Patriarchate at Byzantium in direct opposition to the Roman claim to Peter as first Bishop of Rome. As it has been demonstrated in very great detail, this claim was completely unknown in the Latin West, and in the Greek, Syriac, Coptic, Arabic, and Ethiopic East before the datable text of Nikephoras about 1026. Yet only the Greek and Syriac Churches ever recognized this claim.

The ancient and medieval churches were not content to use Andrew as merely an anti-Peter. The Gnostics and Manichaeans used the apocryphal "Acts of Andrew" to oppose the canonic teaching of the New Testament. Some of this Gnostic-Manichaean teaching is still to be found in the "Acts of Andrew and Matthias". From the time of the appearance of the "Acts of Peter and Andrew" the legends of the apocryphal New Testament become mere miracle stories.

Andrew as a figure in Christian art make a rather late appearance. Usually only the New Testament Andrew is portrayed. Not until the tenth century does any artistic representation of the "Acts of Andrew" appear. In the Greek East only the crucifixion is ever given, while in the Latin West, Gregory's censored version was more widely used. In the Afro-Asian Churches, which produced such a wealth of miracle stories about Andrew, *not* one artistic fragment has survived or been described.

We must assume, then, that Andrew was used from the earliest times as a propaganda figure but that no historic reality (outside of

Mark-Acts) lies behind the legends. Paul and Peter, and possibly the two disciples called James, were important enough to make an impression on the early church or Josephus. Of the original "Twelve", only these four lived or died in such a way that they can be identified as individuals. All the others, whether of the Seventy or of the Twelve, have failed to do this. Like thousands of other Unknown Soldiers in the Church Militant, Andrew lived and died. His personality, teachings, and "identity are known only to God."

APPENDIX: SELECT TEXTS

One of the longest of the Byzantine texts is the *Narratio*; its interest is not in the least diminished by its open use of other material. We quote from section 4 on, the first three sections being only a résumé of the New Testament Andrew.

4. The most Blessed and First-Called Andrew, crossing like a falling star from the East to the West, preached in every city Christ to be God's Son. In crossing the province of Bithynia he entered one of its cities, Nicaea by name, where he taught the Savior-Word and performed some miracle, as is the tradition by some historians of that same city; for down by the East Gate, in a snare of the Arch-Evil One, evil spirits sat down and made it unpassable for men. Informed of this, the First-Called went down to the place and drove the spirits out by calling on Christ our God and, having purified the place of their ambush, made it an unhindered way for all wishing to walk by. From there passing over to Thrace and afterwards sailing to Scythia, he came to great Sevastopol, where the rivers Apsaros and Phâsis form an encampment and the interior Ethiopians dwell. He preached everywhere and proclaimed the true faith of our God.

5. Leaving behind the Euxine Sea, he entered a city called Sinope, where the inhabitants are blood-thirsty savages, wilder than beasts in their understanding and disposition, not only against each other but also against every new- and in- comer. Against these last, they were merciless in their savage place, as they were against the Blessed Matthias, as the book has stated, when he happened to go there for the sake of preaching Christ, our True God, and was unharmed by their outrage and shut up under guard. Afterward they were violently brought to justice. Now the Most Holy First-Called of the Apostles, Andrew, when he came by (as is written) in this city, knew that the Apostle Matthias was locked up with other faithful; by prayer he killed the guards and, opening the doors of the prison, brought out the same Apostle and those with him. When he had freed them, they wished to go on.

6. Hearing of this, the inhabitants of that small town, beastlike in their thought, seized the Apostle and dragged him all over the city, putting him to a public torture. They threw him back into prison, thinking that after all that he would die, mostly because he preached the Lord Jesus the Anointed and reproached their inhuman, bestial, untamed state. At that time the Blessed Apostle Andrew prayed that they be punished until they turned their thoughts and reason to tradition of the faith he preached. Approaching some stone statue of a man, he laid his hands and put a seal on it, saying "I tell you, statue, fear the sign of the cross and pour water until the very harsh inhabitants of this city are punished and turn themselves to the knowledge and faith of the True God, the Father and His Only-Begotten Son and the Life-Giving Spirit."

7. And immediately there came out water from the mouth of the statue

49

in flood-like quantity. The city's inhabitants watched it go higher and higher and knew that it was because of their mistreatment of the Apostle. Running to the prison with great weeping and trembling, they fell before the Apostle and begged him to stop such a threatening ruin and give them the Light of the Anointed's faith. Seeing their sincere conversion and repentance, and feeling merciful, the First-Called said to the statue, "No more let water come out of your mouth, for see, I come to preach to this people the faith of my Lord and God and Savior, Jesus the Anointed." This said, immediately the water's flow stopped. At that time the Apostle came out of the prison, instructed and taught them, and baptised, and founded a church. Staying there seven days, he enlightened them with, and confirmed them in, the faith of the Anointed.

8. From there he went away along the coast of the same Euxine Sea, which flows towards Byzantium, and he proceeded on the right-hand side. He settled at a town called Argyropolis and founded there a church. He laid his hands on one of the Seventy Disciples, by name Stachys, (whom the Apostle Paul, the Anointed's mouth, the body of the élite, mentioned in his Epistle to the Romans as his "beloved") and ordained him bishop of Byzantium. He preached the Savior-Word but went away because of the prevailing idolatrous godlessness there and because of the cruelty of the tyrannous and idol-mad Zeuxippos, who sat in that place in state. He went to the western parts and enlightened with his godly teaching even the western darkness.

9. Going thru Thessaly and Greece, he founded in these cities the mystery of the grace of God's Anointed and went on to Achaia. In a city there called Patrae where the light had not shone, he taught them to reject Hellenism's darkness while resorting to Christianity's light, to take off idolatrous vanity while putting on true righteousness, to detest the deceitful sacrifice of falsely-called gods while worshipping the True God in Trinity and Unity and resorting to piety in the nature of the convert, to go away from the glory of evil demons while coming to the glorified faith of God's Son, to deny all Greek boastings and customs while affirming the teachings that the True God's Anointed became a Man in the flesh by the grace of His birth in the Virgin.

10. Discussing these matters daily with the people, he persuaded them by his teaching to resort to the bath of immortality and to be born again thru God's baptism and to serve the Anointed he preached, Who is God with His Co-existent and Co-ruling Father and the All-Holy Spirit. Among them was the wife of the proconsul at that time, Aegeates, who excelled all men in his cruel and bestial temper. Andrew persuaded her to spit on the Greek holy things and together with her relative Ēphidamia to resort to the preaching of the correct faith of the Christians.

11. Informed of these matters, Aegeates was moved to a rage by the unclean demon which dwelled in him, and, seizing the Blessed One, locked him in prison near the sea. He threatened him repeatedly with all forms of tortures unless Andrew would persuade his wife Maximilla to resume Hellenism and her wifely duties. Altho Andrew was imprisoned, some of the people he had taught used to come to the prison and to hear his words,

including Maximilla. For the Blessed First-Called taught them saying,
[Here Narratio parallels or quotes V.].

12. (= V. section 1 but censored) "My children, you who live after
Christ, our True God, because of our preaching, believe in Him. Above all,
keep His faith unshaken and unmoved permanently in you. Inscribe the
mystery of His grace on the surface of your hearts (cf. 2 Cor. 3 : 3). Stay
steadfast and unmoved (cf. 1 Cor. 15 : 58). Be firm and certain. Neither
by temptation nor by a spirit of error (cf. 1 John 4 : 6) let yourselves be
carried away, and return not to Hellenism; but forever keep in mind the
redemption, which our Savior Himself obtained for us at the cost of His
blood, and keep away from the devil's error and worship. Until your deaths,
keep—never deny—the Name and the Seal with which you have been
sealed. Do not become soft because of deceitful Aegeates' treacherous
flatteries nor be afraid of his reputed tortures. Fear not the punishments,
with which a little while ago he threatened me, but fear rather that which
is prepared for him and for his father the devil and for all those serving
him in idolatry—the unquenchable fire of Gehenna (Mark 9 : 43) and the
gnashing of teeth (Matth. 8 : 12 etc.) and the unresting worm (Mark 9 : 48).
For Aegeates' things are as transitory as a spider's web dissolving, but these
latter things are unending and eternal for those living wickedly and not
remaining believers in the True God."

13. (= V, section 2) Having said these things, Andrew gave orders to
and bade farewell to the brothers and sent each to his own affairs, saying
to them, "I am not being taken away from you, children; but I will be
with you spiritually even tho I am leaving the body in Christ because of
my love for Him." And so, having embraced him, the brothers went away
from the prison. When enough days had gone by, some of the brothers,
together with Maximilla and Ephaidamia, came to the First-Called who was
still in prison and were strengthened and instructed by his teaching: to have
hope in the Lord Jesus Christ and unceasingly to remember that good
things are dependent upon those loving Him and fighting for their confession of Him. So rejoicing and happy, they went away, each to his own
home.

14. Once, when sitting in judgment, Aegeates came to think of the
Most Blessed Apostle Andrew, for he was deeply hurt and incensed over his
wife's separation from him, as she had abandoned him to stay with the
Apostle. He rose up from the judgment seat, and hurried quickly to the
praetorium in order to persuade Maximilla with flatteries and fawnings to
return again to him in (conjugal) union as before. Now Maximilla came from
the prison, where she had been at that time sitting and hearkening to the
words of the First-Called, for she gladly heard him talking his saving words.
She met the proconsul coming into the house, who seeing her said:

15. (= V. section 4) "Maximilla, what about your parents, who pledged
you in marriage to me, not even thinking of my present rank? For they
did not look to wealth or fame or ancestry, but to the good disposition
of my soul and thus decided to join me to you. Now I hold you to be the
lady and mistress of our whole life, and am well-disposed towards you,
and reasonable because of the kindnesses and honors of your generous

parents and because of your love. Why have you done this—to leave my companionship and to cling to that stranger and vagabond? Please return to me. Come with me as before. Let us enjoy each other's love as it was from the beginning; for, in order to give you this advice, I have even abandoned my duty of judging. If you are persuaded by my desires, we shall live together in our old loving ways, and I shall release for your sake the condemned stranger I have in prison. But, if you do not wish to be persuaded by my admonitions, which I, ashamed, put to you, I will still never do anything harsh to you, for I could not if I wished, remembering your former love and affection. But, as for him, whom I have in chains and whom you prefer in affection above me, I will destroy him with the most degrading tortures. I will arrange that you can see him in agony and affliction. Consider, woman, which is expedient for you and for me, your being disagreeable or obedient to me. Tomorrow give me your answer about him."

16. (= V. section 5 beginning). When he had said this to his own wife, Aegeates went away to the court. Maximilla, together with Phaidamia, at the usual time, went to the most Blessed Apostle. Laying his hands on her eyes, she repeated to the First-Called everything which had been told her by her husband. Andrew said to her:

17. (= V. sec. 5-7, but greatly censored.) "O my child Maximilla, if you keep my advice and teaching as a firm anchor for your decision and never fall away from the faith of Christ, Do not do that which Aegeates in flattery and deceitful hypocrisy proposed. Do not be defeated by this threats against me, even if he also threatens to do something terrible against you. Do not be shaken by his easy talks, not be weakened by his filthy suggestions. Do not consent to give yourself in copulation with that worshipper of idols, you who have embraced Christ in baptism. Endure his every threat or passing torment as unimportant for us who are ready to resist, thru Christ whom you believe in, each concept of punishment made by that hater of Christ, Aegeates. Endure a little while and see his power for torment and temporary fame be thrown speedily down by and replaced with his destruction and disgrace. As for you; guard your innocence and purity from his his unclean plots and keep your robe, with which you were made a bride, unsullied, unspotted, and undefiled until your last day and breath. The proconsul is permitted to threaten us not only with words but also to carry out his deeds as seems fit to him. Let him deliver me to the beasts of the north, or burn me in the fire, or drown me in the deep, or cut me with a saw, or hang me on a cross—let him know how much is our love because of Christ, before Whom we place no being in honor. For we see Him and long for Him Who has loved us in excess. We shall endure all because of fear of Him and we shall press for Him and share in His Kingdom according to His true promise."

18. (= V. section 10) Now Stratoklēs, Aegeates' brother, who was standing in the prison and hearkening to the words of the First-Called, became confounded because of the advice given by the Blessed Apostle to Maximilla and began to weep and groan unceasingly. Seeing this, the First-Called took his hand said to him,

"Why do you weep without restraint and not cease? Why are you not at ease but groaning? For I look on your constant wailing and I rejoice that I have not spoken in vain; but rather, I have thrown seed on fruitful ground and you, as good farmers, will let it grow to hundredfold fruit in your hearts. Be not anxious and break not your heart."

19. (= V. section 12) Then Stratoklēs answered him, "Think not, O First-Called Apostle, that I continually weep because of something other then yourself; for the words that come from your mouth are like arrows of fire shot in my heart, burning it up, and inclining me to the faith of the Christ you preach and to love for your Blessedness. My thorny and dried up soul is leveled and prepared for the seeds of your saving words. That they sprout up and grow needs your fortunate help, without which nothing can grow up to be made known."

(= V. section 13) The Apostle replied, "Knowing these things, Stratoklēs my child, I am happy that my teaching to you has not been in vain and therefore I glorify my Lord and God on behalf of your faith. But, in order that you may be informed, tomorrow Aegeates delivers me to be crucified, for Maximilla, servant of Christ, will anger the homicidal serpent dwelling in him, whose relative he is. Because she will not submit to him or to the things in his heart, regarding her relationship to him, Aegeates will turn against me."

20. (= V. section 14). Now while these things were being said to Stratoklēs, Maximilla was not present, for she—obedient to the Apostle's former words—went away to the praetorium, having decided to bid farewell to all the things of the world and to belong as a bride to God alone. Now Aegeates asked her concerning the same matters he had deemed fit to demand before, namely, if she wished to lie with him as of old. She rejected him, not giving in to his speech. The proconsul went away for the time being, to put the Apostle to death. Aegeates considered the kinds of death by which he could take away Andrew's life; and, at the suggestion of his homicidal and misanthropic father the devil, he decided upon a public crucifixion. He then went to breakfast with stomach-slaves of his own kind, with whom he ate like a wild beast devouring innocent flesh. Meanwhile, Maximilla together with Ēphaidamia went again to the prison for the Most Blessed Andrew and found a great crowd of his disciples gathered, while the Apostle taught them:

21. (= V. sections 15 to end, highly condensed and censored). "My brothers and children I have been sent by my Lord to all the world, to preach His miracles, His becoming a Man, His sufferings, His resurrection from the dead, and His ascension to Heaven. I came, according to His will, to you dwelling in these climates, to remind you how vain to serve the falsely-called gods, how futile to honor them, and yet to turn you to knowledge of the God Who exists. I consider those hearkening to my teachings to be blessed, when they abominate the service of idols and recognize His Godship, thru Which all being has obtained existence. I beg you to build on this foundation, which we have given you, as on something unshaken and uninfluenced by anything evil. Guard the standards I have given you, and inscribe my words in your mind. Be firm in your confession of Him.

Be not troubled by what Aegeates does to me, for as God's servant I must undergo this."

(From here to the end, Narratio parallels, and usually has a fuller text than, Martyrium Andreae II, Text A, rarely B; the longer Greek version of the Latin Epistle; and the Passio, abbreviated as in section 6 of this book).

22. (= Mart. II, A, section 1). When Andrew had talked the whole night to the brothers and had prayed with them, early in the morning the Proconsul Aegeates sent for him from the prison and said, "Foreigner! Alien to our people! Human enemy of the fortune of the gods! Foe of all my house! Why have you thought it good to come against us? Why have you made love to my wife to seduce her from my good will and to serve your God? For what reason have you done this against me and against all Achaia? Therefore I shall, cheerfully and joyfully in my leisure, re-pay you for the gift you have given me!" Aegeates commanded him to be scourged and delivered him over for crucifixion, ordering the executioners not to pierce his legs when they hanged him that he might be legally tortured.

23. (= Mart. II, A, section 2). Meanwhile the report went thru all Patrae how the righteous slave of Christ, whom Aegeates put in chains, was being crucified, altho innocent. With one mind they ran together to the sight, for they were angry with Aegeates because of the impiety of his judgment. Now as the executioners were leading Andrew to his place of death, Stratoklēs learned of the event and by running overtook them. He saw the Blessed One violently dragged by the executioners like some evil-doer to a court. Unsparingly beating them and ripping their coats to pieces, he pulled away the First-Called, saying, "You men, recognize me and know, that, only because of this Apostle who taught me to be free from anger and to refrain from excessive wrath, I have not shown you (the difference between) evil Aegeates' plans and the powers of God's servant, Stratoklēs." He took the hand of the Apostle and went with him to the seaside place where the execution was to take place.

24. (= Mart. II, A, section 3); Now the soldiers who had received Andrew from the proconsul left the Apostle with Stratoklēs and returned and told Aegeates, saying, "As we were talking with Andrew, Stratoklēs interfered and ripped our coats and pulled him away from us and took him with him, and see, he left us standing as you see us." Aegeates answered them, "Put on other clothes, and go and fulfill my command to you upon the condemned Andrew. Do not let Stratoklēs see you, and, if he does anything, give him no answer, because if he is angered, he will not even spare me." They did immediately what Aegeates had commanded.

25. (= Mart. II, A, section 3 continued). Now as Stratoklēs came with the Apostle to the appointed place, the former was angry, cursing Aegeates in a low voice; but the Apostle said to him, "No, Stratoklēs, my child. I do not ever want you to be as you are now, but rather you should be above vanity, gentle, humble, not giving evil for evil but being mindful of the Lord's words (cf. Matthew 5 : 39 f) 'If someone strikes you on the right cheek, turn to him your left. As for him who wishes to take your coat, give him your shirt.' We brothers must follow the burdens laid down by the Lord. Let us strip for action and abandon the exterior man to those

who want him. Let us hasten to renew the interior man to give him to God, Who has our whole heart."

26. (= Mart. II, A, section 4 and Mart. I, section 13 end). And as he spoke this and yet more to Stratoklēs and those with them on the way, they came to the place where he was to be executed. Seeing the cross set up at the edge of the seashore's sand, he left them all and went to the cross and spoke to it in a loud voice as if it had a soul.

27. (parallels, abridges, or replaces L section 46; Mart. I, section 14; Ep. Gr. section 10). "Hail, O cross, for you are excelling in joy for all and a truly great rejoycing for the race of men because on you was tied God's Word! Hail, O life-giving cross, most happy and victorious weapon of Him Who, stretched on you, thus wished to save me, a mere man! Hail, O cross, who grieved because Christ was bound on you and who sweetened (life for) His first-created thru His food and who called back the deceived to their ancient eternal life! Hail, O cross, thru whom the robber dwells in paradise and the cherubim prepared his entrance! Hail, O cross, thru whom the race of men has first regained its ancient worth! Hail, O cross, for on you was raised high the All-Highest Father's Most High Only-Begotten Son, Who too raised on high the once in Hell bodies of men! Hail, O cross, upon you I shall depart from this earthly form and, if really worthily the Master's slave, I shall be raised by common death to share His eternity!"

28. (= Ep. Gr. section 11). And when the Blessed Andrew had so spoken, he stood and looked at the cross. Then, turning and coming to the brothers standing by, he ordered the executioners to do what had been commanded them, for those charged with his crucifixion had been standing afar off. (From here, = section 47 and Mart. I section 15). They came and only bound his feet and hands nailing neither of them, nor piercing his legs, for so the proconsul had ordered. This wretched man wished to torture yet more the righteous one in this way so that the dogs would come and eat him alive in the night. So they left him hanging and went away.

29. (= Ep. Gr. section 11; Mart. II, A, section 5). Now the multitudes which he had made disciples in Christ were standing by and, seeing what they did to Andrew was not normal for crucifixions, they hoped to hear something from him. The Saint, as he hanged there, moved his head and smiled. So Stratoklēs asked him saying, "Why do you smile, First-Called of God's slaves? Are you smiling because we mourn to be deprived of you?" The Apostle answered, "Shall I not laugh, Stratoklēs, when I think of the futile attacks of Aegeates? For he does not even know that crucifixion is the greatest honor for us, nor does he know that we cannot be punished because of our love for Christ." And by way of answer, he lectured to the people:

30. (= Ep. Gr., section 11, which has a shorter version). "You men who are standing around, and you women and children, old and young, slaves and free men, listen to me, and take no heed for the vain deceit of this present life, but rather pay attention to us, hanging here for the Lord's sake and ready to leave this body. Renounce all the worldly lusts and spit upon the worship of the abominable idols. Run instead to the true worship of our never-lying God and make yourselves a temple pure and ready to receive the Word, Who together with His Father and the Holy Spirit

shall come and prepare a mansion for you (cf. John 14 : 23). Shake off indolence and gloom from your hearts and take on virtuous industry and enlightenment in your souls. Be awake and stand, having girded your loins in cheerfulness. Put on your chest a spiritual breastplate. (Cf. Eph. 6 : 14 ff) Having drawn the sword of the Word, cut off the fleshly lusts from your hearts and become pure and perfect, undefiled and unspotted, because or our pure God. Purify yourselves and do not forget my teachings; for, because of them, you have become heirs—not because of your human eye or ear or heart—heirs of every good gift taken and prepared by our God for those who love Him forever (cf. I Cor 2 : 9)."

31. (= Ep. Gr. section 12; Mart. II, A., section 6; P section 5). The Apostle continued to speak so for a day and a night, while hanging from the cross, and the people gladly listened. Then seeing his endurance and constancy of soul and wisdom of spirit, and strength of mind, they were all angry and hurried away to the judgment seat, where they shouted against Aegeates, saying, "An evil decision, Proconsul! You have ill judged! You have condemned unjustly! Your court is illegal! Unrighteously you persecute all Achaia! You have acted unworthily against that righteous man! For what wrong has he done? What unjust act? What sin has he committed? You have been unjust to all of us! All the city is troubled. All the people are worried. Do not kill the righteous one! Be merciful to that man for our sake! Kill not a pious man! He has been hanging for two days and is still alive! He has tasted not food and yet he refreshes us with his words. See, we believe in the God he preaches. Take down the righteous man and we will all be philosophers. Free the chaste man so that all Patrae will be at peace! Release the wise man and all Achaia will be freed by him!"

32. (same as 31). Now when at first Aegeates would not listen to them, for he had no desire to release the righteous man to the crowd, he simply waved his hand that they would leave the judgment seat. The crowd became very angry and fell upon him and were about to do him harm, for there were about two thousand of them. The proconsul became a madman, but wishing no uprising against himself, he rose from his judgment seat and went off, promising to free the righteous Andrew. Someone went ahead and indicated to the Apostle and to the people standing around why the proconsul was coming. As he was arriving, the whole crowd of the disciples, including Maximilla and Ēphaidamia and Stratoklēs, rejoiced.

33. (same as 31). But when Andrew heard it, he began to say, "O the dullness and disobedience and simplicity of my disciples! How much have I spoken and they still are not persuaded to flee from the love of earthly things! But they are still bound to them and continue in them and will not depart from them. What does this love and lust and longing for the flesh mean? How long will you care for worldly and transient things? How long will you not understand the things above us, and not hurry to overtake them? From now on, let me be killed in the way you now see me. Let no man whatever free me from these bonds, for it is so fated me that I now depart from the body and be present with the Lord, with Whom I am being crucified. And this shall be accomplished."

34. (= L section 48 and Ep. Gr. 13). And turning, he said to Aegeates, "O Proconsul, why have you come again to us? What are you seeking that you overtake even me? Why have you come, you alien enemy of mine? What are you planning to do? What is your new dare? To free us from these bonds, and in this expectation, we should fall into your trap? But you shall not loosen us. Aegeates! Nor shall you bring us down! Not even if you promised all your goods to us, would we believe you! For all your temporal goods are going to be destroyed with you! Nor do I fear any of your threats! For my Lord Jesus Christ has Himself appeared to me, saying, 'Understand Aegeates and fear not from him, altho he is terrible, a destroyer, hateful, a deceiver, a corrupter, a madman, a sorcerer, a cheat, a murderer, wrathful and unmerciful. Venom of asps is from his lips (cf. Rom. 3 : 13); his garment is like a wolf's skin. He is bestial-minded and a killer of men, truly, his father from the beginning was Satan.' Therefore, I recognize you, by virtue of the God Who never lies and Who so informed me. I shall escape you by going to the righteous Judgment. Well I know that you will be cut off and be grieved and unhappy when you see yourself thrown into the fire of Gehenna, which has been prepared for you and your fellow-worshippers of your father the devil."

35. (= Ep. Gr. section 14 and P 6). But the proconsul, on hearing this, stood speechless and, as it were, beside himself; but as all the city made an uproar to make him free Andrew, he dared approach the cross to free him. But the Apostle with a great voice shouted to Heaven, "Do not allow, Master, that I, now bound to the cross, be taken down again. Deliver me not who am on Thy mystery to the shameless devil. O Jesus, God's Son, do not let me, who suffer as Thou didst, be taken down. O Father, Son, and Holy Spirit, protect those here who have seen Thy glory, and who long for, love, and believe in Thee because of our preaching. Keep them safe from the enemy demon and make them sure in Thy faith and give them the grace to worship and glorify Thee, our true God. O Jesus Christ, Whom I have seen, do have and love, to Whom even I do and shall belong, take me in peace into Thy eternal tents. May my going out become a going into Thee by the many, akin to me, who rest in Thy majesty." Having so spoken and all the more glorified the Lord, he gave up the ghost, while everybody wept and lamented at his parting.

36. (= P section 7; L section 49; Ep. Gr. section 15; Mart. I section 18, and II, A and B, section 10). After the passing away of his blessed ghost, Maximilla, paying no attention to any of the bystanders, stepped forward and herself took down the body of the Blessed Andrew, First-Called of the Apostles. Having given it the usual care, she buried it on the sea-shore, where the prison is. She remained separate from Aegeates because of his bestial mind and lawless manner of living. Aegeates pleaded much with her and promised that she would be the ruler and mistress in all his affairs, but she never weakened and resisted strongly. Moreover, she led a pious and quiet life, together with her Ēphaidamia, and continued to serve the Apostle and minister to the brothers until her last breath. As he could not persuade her, the proconsul suffered greatly and became a madman. One night, standing up in silence, he threw himself down from

a very tall place of his praetorium, and so he perished, just as the Apostle foresaw and prophesied.

37. (same as 36, and Mart. II, section 11). Now Stratoklēs, his brother, did not wish to touch any of Aegeates' possessions, for the wretched man died childless; but said: "Let your goods perish with you, Aegeates, for of these things we have no need whatever, as they are defiled." (From here on, 37 is peculiar only to N). "But as for me, let Christ be my Friend and I His slave. All my possessions I offer to Him in Whom I have believed. I pray that by worthy hearing of the blessed teaching of the Apostle I may appear a participant with him in the ageless and endless Kingdom." And so the uproar of the people ceased and all were glad at the amazing and untimely and sudden death of the impious and most lawless Aegeates.

38. (The date is given at the end of all the texts giving the death of Andrew.) Now the Holy and First-Called Apostle Andrew died on the 30 November, in the Kingship of our Lord Jesus Christ, to Whom be the Glory and the Power together with the Father and the All-Holy Spirit, now and forever and until the ages of ages. Amen. [1]

The "Acts of Andrew and Matthias" have never been translated from the original Greek into English, nor does Hennecke take the trouble to translate this, the best-known, legend of Andrew into German. For this reason, the following pages give the most important passages verbatim, and at least a résumé of the less interesting.

The beginning presents the interesting theory that the Apostles on Pentecost drew lots to decide their mission fields, an item mentioned frequently in the lists of the Apostles cited above. The story is sufficiently short so that the whole of the section dealing with Andrew may be given here. Matthias (often called Matthew in some texts) is given the City of Cannibals as his lot. After he has arrived, he is blinded, given a drug which fails to affect him, and is thrown into prison. Jesus appears and tells him that Andrew is coming to save him, to arrive in twenty-seven (Syriac, twenty-five) days.

"4. When the twenty-seven days were completed after Matthew's imprisonment, the Lord appeared in the country in which Andrew was teaching and said to him, 'Rise and go with your disciples to the Country of the Cannibals and take Matthias out of that place, for three days more, and the men of the City are going to take him out and kill him for their food.' And answering, Andrew said, 'My Lord, I am not able to go there in the space of three days, but send quickly Thy angel to take him out of there. For Thou knowest, Lord, that I am flesh and cannot go there quickly. Moreover, I do not know the way.' And He answered Andrew, 'Listen to your Maker, to the Word Who can speak and that city is transplanted here and all its inhabitants. I command the wings of the winds and they shall take it from there. But, getting up early, go to the sea with your disciples and you will find a ship on the shore and you will go aboard with your disciples.' Saying these things, the Savior again spoke, 'Peace upon you, Andrew, and those with you.' And He went up into Heaven.

---

[1] End of Narratio.

"5. Now, having gotten up early, Andrew went to the sea with his disciples, and, going along the shore, saw a little ship, and on the ship three men sitting. For the Lord in His own power had prepared a ship and He was like a human pilot in the ship, and He had two angels, whom He made appear like men and they were sitting with Him in the ship. Then Andrew, seeing the ship and the three men in it, rejoiced with a great joy, and, going to them, he said, 'Where are you going to in this small boat, brothers?' And answering, the Lord said to him, 'We go to the City of the Cannibals'. Now Andrew, seeing Jesus, did not recognize Him, for Jesus had hidden His Divinity and appeared to Andrew as a human pilot. But Jesus, hearing Andrew say 'I am going to the City of the Cannibals, too,' replied, 'Every man flees that city. Why do you go there?' Answering, Andrew said, 'We have to carry out a small matter there, and we must finish it. But, if possible, do us this kindness, to take us to the Country of the Cannibals, where you also are going to travel.' Answering, Jesus said, 'Come on board.'

"6. Andrew said, 'I wish to make one thing clear to you before we board your ship.' Said Jesus, 'Say what you please.' Andrew said to Him, 'We have no shiphire to pay you, nor have we bread to eat.' Answering, Jesus said to him, 'How do you (expect to) come aboard since you have neither shiphire nor bread to eat?' But Andrew said to Jesus, 'Listen, Brother, do not think that because of any tyranny in us, we do not give you our ship money; but we are disciples of Our Lord Jesus the Anointed, the good God. For he chose us Twelve and gave us this commandment: Going out to preach, do not take silver on the way, nor bread, nor a purse, nor sandals, nor a staff, nor two coats. [1] If, then, you will do this kindness for us, tell us quickly, or make clear to us and we will go away and see another boat for ourselves.' Answering, Jesus said to Andrew, 'If that is the commandment which you have received and you honor it, come aboard My ship with all joy. For, truly, I prefer that you, the disciples of Him called Jesus, come aboard my ship than those carrying gold and silver, because I am really worthy that the Apostle of the Lord comes aboard my ship.' Answering, Andrew said, 'Permit me, Brother, may the Lord grant you glory and honor.' Andrew and his disciples went on the ship.

"7. And going in, (Andrew) sat in the middle of the ship. And Jesus said to one of the angels, 'Get up and go to the belly of the ship and bring three loaves of bread, that the men may eat and not go hungry because of the long trip they made to us. Going below, he brought up from the belly of the ship three loaves as the Lord commanded and set the three loaves before them. At that time Jesus said to Andrew, 'Stand up, brother, together your own men. Take the bread as food so that you may be strong to cross the waves of the sea.' Answering, Andrew said to his disciples, 'My children, we have found a great act of human kindness by this man. Stand up, then, take this bread as food so that you will be strong to cross the waves of the sea.' His disciples could not answer him a word, for they were sea-sick. Then Jesus forces Andrew to eat bread with his disciples. Andrew said to Jesus, not knowing that it was Jesus, "Brother, the Lord

---

[1] Matthew 10 : 10; Luke 10 : 4.

shall give you heavenly food from His Kingdom. Let us alone, brother, for you see that the children are quite sea-sick.' Jesus answered Andrew, 'Certainly the brothers are unused to the sea; but allow them, if they wish, to go on land you remain until your duty is completed and you go again to them.' At that time Andrew told his disciples, 'My children, do you wish to go on land while I remain here to finish the duty commanded me?' They answered Andrew, 'If we are away from you, we become strangers to the good things which the Lord has given us. Now, therefore, we are with you wherever you go.'

"8. Jesus said to Andrew, 'If truly you are a disciple of Him called Jesus, tell your disciples of the mighty deeds which your Teacher did so that their souls may rejoice and lose their fear of the sea, for, see, we are going to free the ship from the land! Immediately Jesus told one of the angels, 'Loosen the ship'. And he loosened the ship from the land. Jesus went and sat at the rudder and piloted the ship. [Andrew tells his disciples of the stilling of the storm by Jesus.] [1] And having said these things, Andrew prayed in his heart that his disciples would fall asleep; and while Andrew prayed, the disciples fell asleep." Now that the reader has seen the style of the text, with its enormously repetative style, the translation will continue; but the repetitions shall be paraphased in (. . .).

"9. Now Andrew turned to the Lord, not knowing that it was the Lord, and said to Him, 'Tell me, Man, how you pilot the ship, for I have never seen a man piloting a ship as I now see you. For sixteen years I have sailed the sea, this is my seventeenth, and I have never seen such a method. Truly, this ship is as on land. Show me, Youth, your method.' Jesus answered him, 'Many times we sailed the sea and were in danger; but, because you are the disciple of Him called Jesus, the sea knows that you are righteous and is quiet and throws not her waves against the ship.' Then Andrew cried out with a loud voice, 'Bless Thee, my Lord Jesus the Anointed, that I meet a man who glorifies Thy name.'

"10. Jesus (asked) Andrew, 'Tell me, disciple of Him called Jesus, why the faithless Jews did not believe Him and say He is not God but a Man. Explain (. . .) for we hear that he showed His Divinity to His disciples.' Andrew (replied), 'Truly, He showed to us that He is God, for He made the sky and the earth and the sea and all in them.' Jesus (asked), 'Why did not the Jews believe? Certainly he performed signs for them.' (Andrew tells of some of the New Testament miracles, but Jesus insists on knowing even more.) [2]

"11. Andrew (replied), 'Yes, Brother, He did (miracles) even before the High Priests, not only in public but in secret, and they did not believe Him.' Jesus answered, 'What miracles did He do secretly? Explain to me! (Reluctantly Andrew begins to tell in 12.)

" 'Once we Twelve went with Our Lord to a heathen temple, so that He might show us the ignorance of the devil, and the high priest, seeing us follow Jesus, said to us: " "O you stupidest men! How can you walk

---

[1] Matthew 8 : 23-27, Mark 4 : 36-41, Luke 8 : 23 ff.
[2] Namely, Matthew 11 : 5, John 2 : 1-10, Matthew 15 : 14 ff.

with One who says,' 'I am the God's Son' ', Does God have a Son? Which of you ever saw God talking with a woman? Is He not the son of Joseph the carpenter and his mother is Mary and his brothers James and Simon[1]?" " When we heard these things, our hearts turned to weakness. But Jesus knew how our hearts leaned and took us to a desert place where He performed great signs before us and showed us His Divinity. We told those high priests, " "Come and see, for he has convinced us." "

" '13. (They come and) Jesus showed them what Heaven is (Here is a story from another source, as the abrupt beginning shows. Perhaps it is from the Acts of Andrew.).... that we might learn whether it were true or not. Thirty men from the people and four high priests came with us. Jesus saw two carved sphinxes, one on the right, one on the left, of the temple. And turning, Jesus said to us, " "See the form of Heaven, for such are the cherubim and the seraphim in Heaven." " Then looking at the sphinx at the right, Jesus said, " "Model of that in Heaven, even tho made by artisans, come down and convince these priests whether I be Man or God." "

"14. The sphinx came down and spoke with a human voice, " "O foolish sons of Israel! You who are not only blown up by the blindness of your hearts but wish to blind others like yourselves in saying that God is a man. This is He Who in the beginning made mankind and gave him breath, the Mover of all Immoveable. This is He Who called Abraham, Who loved Isaac, his son, Who threw His beloved Jacob to the ground, Who made the living and the dead, the Maker of all good things for His believers and of punishments for the unbelievers. Do not say to me that I am only a carved idol, for I tell you that the temples are better than your synagogue. Our priests who serve in this temple clean themselves because they fear the demons; for, whenever they go with women, they clean themselves seven days on account of this fear and come not in the temple because of us, because of the name which God gave us. But you, whenever you fornicate, take God's law and go into God's synagogue and sit and read and are not pious concerning God's glorious words. Therefore, I say to you that the temples will replace your synagogues so that they become even Churches (*ekklesía*) of His Only-Begotten Son." " When the sphinx had said these things, the High Priests were silent.

"15. We told the High Priest that they (the stones—*hoi líthoi?*) were worthy to be believed, " "Even the stones tell you the truth and disgrace you." " [Up to this point, the Greek of the text of this unusual episode was of a higher type than found elsewhere in the AM. The repetitions are absent, the vocabulary contains rarer words, e.g., *pnoé* instead of *pneûma*, while a dogma of an anti-Jewish and anti-sexual nature appears, not unlike that of the AA.]

(The High Priests reply that it was only magic) " "Did not the stone say that He spoke with Abraham? How could He have spoken with or seen Abraham?" " (Jesus asks the sphinx to) " "Go to the land of the Canaanites and to the cave of Mambrê field ,where is the body of Abraham, [2] and call

---

[1] Matthew 13 : 55, *not* Mark 6 : 3.
[2] Genesis 23 : 9, 17; 25 : 9 f; 35 : 27; 49 : 30 f.; 50 : 13.

from outside the memorial "Abraham, Abraham, whose body is in the memorial, but whose soul is in Paradise, the Maker of man in the beginning, and Who made you His friend, says to come with your sons Isaac and Jacob to the temple of the Jebusaeans, so that we may convict the High Priests so that they know that I knew you and you knew Me." (The Twelve Patriarchs come by mistake and Jesus has to send again for the Three, who convict the High Priests. The latter still do not believe. Andrew concludes, saying that Jesus performed many other miracles.)

(16. Jesus causes Andrew to sleep and orders his angels to place the Apostle and his disciples outside the City of the Cannibals. They do so and Jesus and his angels return to Heaven.)

"17. Dawn having come, Andrew awoke from his sleep and found himself lying on the ground. Looking around, he saw the gates of the city and his disciples lying asleep on the ground. He told them, 'My children, stand up and know the great grace which the Lord did for us, and know that it was the Lord in the ship with us and we did not recognize Him." (The disciples tell Andrew of their great dream in which they saw the Lord in Heaven with the Twelve Apostles, each of whom is served by an angel.)

"18. Then Andrew, hearing these thing from his disciples, rejoiced with a great joy because his disciples were worthy of seeing the greatness of God. He lifted up his eyes to Heaven, praying, 'Pardon me, Lord Jesus the Anointed, and forgive what I have done. For as a man I saw Thee in the ship and as a man I spoke with Thee. Now, Lord, show Thyself to me in this place.' Jesus appeared to Andrew in the form of a very handsome and very young boy and said, 'Andrew, Our own, hail!' (Andrew, falling to the ground worshipped Him, and asked:) 'What was my sin, Lord Jesus, that Thou didst not show Thyself to me on the sea?' (Jesus tells Andrew that it was only because Andrew doubted being able to reach Cannibal City in three days. Moreover, Andrew is to rescue Matthias but will be tortured later by the people.)

"19. Andrew stands up and goes into the city with his disciples, and no one sees them. They come to the prison (which is guarded by seven men) and he prays and the seven guards, falling down on the ground, give up the ghost. Going up to the door, Andrew makes the sign of the cross and the door automatically opens. Entering the prison with his disciples, Andrew sees Matthias sitting and singing by himself, who stands up on seeing the former and they greet with a holy kiss. [1] (Andrew says to Matthew): "How are you going to escape from here? For in three days they are going to kill you and use you as food in this city. Where are the holy mysteries which you learned? Where are the miracles which we believe and by which Heaven is removed and the earth trembles?' (Matthias quotes Matthew 10 : 16, where Jesus sends the disciples like sheep among the wolves and that Jesus had appeared and promised to send Andrew to help him.)

"20. Andrew, looking around through the prison, saw men lying naked and eating grass, as speechless beasts. Striking his breast, Andrew

[1] Cf. Romans 16 : 16.

said within himself, 'O Andrew, what has happened to these men who are like you? How have they been made into unthinking beasts?' (Andrew began to curse Satan:) "Woe to you, Enemy of God and His Angels, that nothing has happened to you as to these strangers! How have you brought them to this honor? How long do you war against the race of men? For you made Adam be thrown out of Paradise; [1] and God gave him grain to sow on the ground, while you made the very bread on his table change to stones. [2] Again it was you who entered the minds of the angels and made them to be defiled with women and made their sons the giants [3] into savages so that they ate men on the earth until God sent the flood on them in His anger, wiping out all that the Lord had erected (except His righteous Noah). You come in this city and make them to eat men so that their end will be damnation and perdition, for you think within yourself that God will wipe out His creation. Or do you know that God promised " "I will not make a flood again on the earth" "? [4] But what is preparing a punishment for your deeds?'

"21. At that time Andrew and Matthias stood up and prayed, Andrew laying hands on the heads of the blind prisoners. Immediately they all could see. Again he laid his hand on their hearts and their minds were changed to human reason. Then Andrew told them, 'Go to the lower part of the city and find there a big fig tree and eat of its fruits until I come to you. And if I delay in coming to you, you will find enough fruit on it to be your food (no matter how much you may eat. 'The men beg Andrew to come with them in their fear for the cannibals, but he tells them to go on) 'for not even a dog will lift up his tongue against you.' There were two hundred seventy men and forty-nine women, whom Andrew released from the prison. The men went just as the blessed Andrew told them. He made Matthias go with his disciples to the east side of the city and (ordered a cloud to take them to the mountain where Peter was teaching).

"22. Andrew went out from the prison and walked thru the city and, seeing a bronze column with a man's statue on it, sat down to see what would happen. When the public executioners went to the prison to bring the men out in order to kill them with a knife for food, they found the doors of the prison open and the guards lying dead on the ground. Immediately they went and announced it to the rulers of the city, 'The prison we found opened and inside nobody but the guards lying dead on the ground.' (The rulers said to bring the bodies of the seven guards for food and to bring the old men of the city to an assembly in which lots would be thrown to find who was to be the next day's food. They would also choose young men to board warships and bring back captives for food. The guards bring the bodies to the center of the city where is a large furnace and a great vat for the blood, upon which they place the men.) As the executioners take their knives in their hands, a voice come to Andrew, 'See, Andrew,

[1] Genesis 3 : 1, 23.
[2] Adam and Eve I : 68??
[3] Genesis 6 : 2-8.
[4] Genesis 9 : 11.

what is happening in the city.' Seeing that, Andrew prayed, 'Lord Jesus
the Anointed, you told me to come to this city. Do not let anything so
evil happen in this city but let the knives go out of the hands of the lawless.'
(It happened) and their hands became stone. (The rulers cried out:) 'Woe
to us for there are magicians here who enter prisons and lead men out. See,
they have even worked magic on these. Go, collect the old men because
we are hungry.'

"23. (They brought two hundred fifteen, of whom seven were selected
by lot. One of the losers said to the rulers,) 'I beg you, I have a very small
son, my very own; take him and eat instead of me and let me alone.' (The
rulers finally agree to accept not only the son but also a daughter. Just before
they are to be killed, Andrew prayed,) 'Lord Jesus the Anointed, just as
you heard my prayer for the dead and did not allow them to be eaten,
so now hear my prayer that the public executioners not kill the children
but that the knives (again fall from their hands.' This happens and the people
are afraid, while Andrew glorifies the Lord).

"(24. The rulers complain and the devil appears in the form of an old
man) and began to speak in middle of the crowd, 'Woe to you, because
you will die for lack of food. What is making you into sheep and cattle?
That is not enough for you! Get up and look for a stranger dwelling in the
city by the name of Andrew and kill him! He is the man who freed the men
from the prison. He is still in the city and you do not know him! Now go
look for him so that you can eat the rest of your food.' Andrew could see
the devil as he spoke to the crowd, but the devil could not see Andrew.
Andrew (told) the devil, 'O Belía, you worst of enemies! You make war
against all creation, but my Lord Jesus the Anointed will humble thee . . . .
into the abyss.' The devil (said,) 'Your voice I hear and I recognize, but I
do not know where you are.' Andrew relied to the devil, 'Why are you
named Amaél? Is it not because you are blind and cannot see the holy
ones?' (The devil tells the citizens to find Andrew but they cannot even see
him). The Lord appeared to Andrew and said, 'Andrew, stand up and show
yourself so that they may learn the power of the devil operating within
them'.

"25. Andrew announces himself before the people, 'See, I am Andrew,
whom you are seeking.' The whole crowd rushes upon him, shouting,
'What you have done to us, we do to you.' (And they debated among themselves,) 'How shall we kill him? If we cut off his head, the death will not be
painful for him. If we roast him in the fire and give his body to ourselves
as food, that death will not be painful enough.' Then, after the devil had
entered and filled his heart, one said, 'As he showed us, so we show him
and we found for him a very evil torture. Let's go tie a rope around his
neck and drag him thru all the streets and lanes of the city every day until
his death. After his death, we give his body to all the citizens as food to
eat.' (So they did) until parts of Andrew's flesh were torn off by the ground
and his blood flowed like water on the ground. When it was evening, they
threw him in the prison, his hands tied behind and his body paralysed.

"26. (The following day they repeated the whole process). The devil
walked behind and told the crowd, "Hit him on the mouth so that he cannot

talk'. [1] (The devil came afterwards to the prison with seven evil demons, whom Andrew had driven out from the neighborhood. [2] [Cf. Gregory, section 6, where Andrew drives seven demons out of a man.] The devil and the demons set up a howl, saying to Andrew,) 'Now you have fallen into our hands. Where now is your power, your fear, your glory, and your pride? You fell into our hands, you who dishonor us, and overthrow our works in town and land, and make our temples desert places so that no one sacrifices to us, as we delight in. Therefore, we are doing the opposite and will kill you just as Herod killed your teacher Jesus.'

"27. The devil (orders) the demons, 'My children, kill this man who dishonors us, so that the rest of the countries become ours.' The seven demons went to Andrew, wishing to kill him; but seeing the seal on his forehead, which the Lord had given, they were greatly afraid, and could not go near him but fled. (The devil rebukes the demons, who reply 'Kill him yourself.' They mock Andrew, who drives them away with the remark) 'If you kill me here, it will not be your will but the will of Him Who sent me, Jesus the Anointed. For that reason you have mocked me, that I shall complete the Lord's commandment. For if the Lord makes me bishop in this city, I shall punish you as you deserve.'

"28. In the morning the people again tie a rope around Andrew's neck and again parts of his flesh were torn by the ground and his blood flowed like water. The blessed one cried out, 'Lord Jesus the Anointed, these tortures are enough, for I am exhausted. Thou hast seen how the enemy mocked me with his demons and Thou art mindful of Thy three days on the Cross when, being little-souled, Thou said" "My Father, why hast Thou forsaken Me" " ' [3] [This part of the AM is surely from the author of the present text; the Gnostic AA could never have had a torture scene or such a reference to Jesus' sufferings.]

'When we walked with Thee, Thou said to us " "They shall not touch one hair of your heads." " [4] (For Thou seest my present tortures). 'At that time a voice said to him in Hebrew, 'Our own Andrew, Heaven and earth will pass away, but My words will not pass away. [5] Look behind.' (Andrew saw fruit-bearing trees growing up where his flesh and blood touched the ground. Thinking that Andrew would die in the night, the people returned him to prison.)

"29. The Lord appeared in the prison and, stretching forth His hand, said, 'Give me your hand, Andrew, and stand up healthy.' (Andrew did and thanked the Lord. In the prison was a pillar and on it the alabaster statue of a man. Andrew spread out his hands seven times and said, 'Fear the sign of the cross and from the mouth of the statue let water pour out in a flood. Say not, I am but a stone, for God made us of earth, but you are clean, and

---

[1] Cf. Acts 23 : 2 f.
[2] Cf. Matthew 12 : 45 and Luke 11 : 26.
[3] Matthew 27 : 46, *not* Mark 15 : 34.
[4] Luke 12 : 18 (a text omitted by Marcion, a pro-Gnostic!)
[5] Matthew 24 : 35 rather than Mark 13 : 31.

therefore God gave his people the law on tables of stone.' (The flood was bitter, corrupting the flesh of men.)

(30. That morning the people began to flee, while their children and cattle died. Andrew prayed that the Archangel Michael would come on a cloud of fire and surround the city. So it happened, and the people rush to the prison to free Andrew shouting 'God of this stranger, take away the water.' Andrew leaves the prison, the water parting before him. 31. The old man who had offered his two children to be eaten came and begged forgiveness.) "Andrew replied, 'I am amazed how you can say " "Have mercy on me," " You did not have mercy on your children, but gave them up to be eaten instead of you. I tell you, at the same hour that the water goes down into the abyss, you and the fourteen executioners, who have murdered men every day, will also go in the abyss and stay in Hell until I return and bring you back up.' (This all occurred. 32. Then he ordered them to bring all the dead, and he brought them to life. He planned a church and baptized the people, giving them the Lord's commandments. They asked Andrew to stay a while longer; but he refused, saying that he must first go to his disciples).

"33. The Lord Jesus came down, taking the form of a little boy (and told Andrew) 'Andrew, why do you go away and let them be no-fruits? Don't you pity the children following you and the men begging you to stay a little while? Now, then go back and I will convert their souls to the Faith, and later you leave the city and go to the city of the barbarians, you and your disciples. After you enter the city, and have preached My Gospel, then bring up the men from the abyss. ' " (Andrew does all this while the people rejoice).

ABBREVIATIONS FOR FOOT-NOTES AND BIBLIOGRAPHY

Bonnet, *Acta* = Lipsius-Bonnet, *Acta Apostolorum Apocrypha*, II,1.
Bonnet, *Sup.* = *Supplementum Codicis Apocryphi*, II.
Lipsius, *Acta* = *Acta Apostolorum Apocrypha*, I .
Lipsius, *Ap.* = *Die Apokryphen Apostelgeschichten und Apostellegenden.*
Hennecke, I = *Hennecke, Neutestamentliche Apokryphen.*
Hennecke, II = *Hennecke, Handbuch zu den Neutestamentlichen Apokryphen.*
PG = *Patrologiae cursus completus, Series graeco-latina*, published by Migne.
PL = *Patrologiae cursus completus, Series latina*, published by Migne.
PW = Pauly-Wissowa (-Kroll), *Realenzyklopädie der Klassischen Altertums-wissenschaft.*
Schermann, *Vitae* = *Prophetarum Vitae Fabulosae Indices Discipulorumque Domini Dorotheo-Epiphanio-Hippolyto Aliisque Vindicata.*
Schermann, *Propheten* = *Propheten- und Apostellegenden nebst Jüngerkatalogen des Dorotheus und verwandter Texte.*
TU = *Texte und Untersuchungen.*

BIBLIOGRAPHY

Abbeloos, Johannes Baptista, et Thomas Joseph Lamy, *Chronicum Ecclesiasticum auctore Bar-Hebrâja*, Louvain, 1872.

Bauer, Walter, *Griechisch-Deutsches Wörterbuch*, 4. Aufl., Berlin, 1952.

Blatt, Franz, *Die lateinische Bearbeitung des Acta Andreae apud anthropophagos*, Beiheft 12 zur *Zeitschrift für die neutestamentliche Wissenschaft*, 1930.

Bonnet, Maximilian, *Supplementum Codicis Apocryphii*, Paris, 1895.

——, "La Passion d'André en quelle langue a-t-elle été écrite?", *Byzantinische Zeitschrift*, III, 1894.

——, *Gregorii Turonensis Liber de Miraculis B. Andreae Apostoli, Scriptores Rerarum Merovingicarum* I, in *Monumenta Germaniae Historica*, 1883.

——, et Richard Adelbert Lipsius, *Acta Apostolorum Apocrypha*, vol. II, Leipzig, 1898.

Budge, Ernest Alfred Wallis, *The Contendings of the Apostles*, vol. I, Oxford, 1899; vol. II, 2nd. edition, 1935.

——, *Salomon of Basra's Book of the Bee in Anecdota Oxoniensis, Semitic Series*, voll. I, 1886.

Chabot, J. B., *Chronique de Michel le Syrien*, Paris, 1899.

Corpus Scriptorum Historiae Byzantinorum.

Cullmann, Oscar, *Peter: Disciple-Apostle-Martyr*, translated by Floyd V. Filson, London and Philadelphia, 1953.

Dalmann, Gustav H., *Aramäisch-Deutsches Wörterbuch*, 3. Aufl., Leipzig, 1938.

Diekamp, F., *Hippolytos von Theben*, Münster, 1898.

Delehaye, H., *Bibliotheca Hagiographica Latina, Graeca, Orientalis*, Brussels, 1895 f (Replaced by Stegmüller, *q.v.*).

Dulaurier, A., *Fragment des Révélations Apocryphes de S. Barthémy*, Paris, 1835.

Eisler, Robert, *Jesous Basileus ou Basileusas*, Leipzig, 1929 f.

Encheiridon Biblicum, Rome, 1955.

Fabricius, Johannes Albert, *Codex Apocryphus Novi Testamenti*, vol. II Hamburg, 1743.

Flamion, Joseph, *Les Actes Apocryphes de l'Apôtre André*, Louvain, 1911.

Gedeōn, Manouēl I., *Patriarchikoi Pinakes*, Thessalonikē and Constantinople, 1885.

Grimm, Jakob, *Andreas und Elene*, Kassel, 1841.

Guidi, Ignazio, *Gli Atti Apocrifi degli Apostoli nei Testi Copti, Arabi, ed Etiopi in Giornale della Società Asiatica Italiana*, vol. II, 1888.

Hatch, Edwin and Henry A. Redpath, *A Concordance to the Septuagint*, Oxford and Graz, Austria, 1897 and 1954.

Harnack, Adolf, *Bruchstücke des Evangeliums und Apokalypse des Petrus*, in *Texte und Untersuchungen*, vol. IX, part 2, Leipzig, 1893.

Hē Theia Leitourgia, Athens: Michaēl I. Saliberou, no date.

Hennecke, Edgar (and others), *Neutestamentliche Apokryphen*, Tübingen, 1904 and 1924.

——, *Handbuch zu den neutestamentlichen Apokryphen*, Tübingen, 1904.

Heussi, Karl, *Kompendium der Kirchengeschichte*, Tübingen, 1910.

James, Montague Rhodes, *The Apocryphal New Testament*, Oxford, 1924.

Lacau, Pierre, *Fragments d'Apocryphes Coptes*, in vol. 9, *Mémoires publiés... de l'Institut Français d'Archéologie Orientale*, Cairo, 1904.

——, und Carl Schmidt, *Gespräche Jesu mit Seinen Jüngern nach der Auferstehung*, in *Texte und Untersuchungen*, vol. 13, III. Reihe, 1919.

Lake, Kirsopp, "Acts (Apocryphal)", *Dictionary of the Apostolic Church*, edited by Hastings, New York, 1915.

Lamy, Thomas Joseph: see Abbeloos,

Latourette, Kenneth Scott, *A History of Christianity*, New York, 1953.

Lietzmann, Hans, *Kleine Texte für Theologische und Philologische Vorlesungen und Übungen*, Bonn, 1903 f. Number 1: *Das Muratorische Fragment*; Number 3: *Apocrypha I — Reste des Petrusevangeliums* (edited E. Klostermann).

Lewis, Agnes Smith, *Horae Semiticae No. III*: *Acta Mythologica Apostolorum*, London 1904.

Liechtenhan, R., *Die Offenbarung im Gnosticismus*, Göttingen, 1901.

——, "*Die Pseudepigraphische Litteratur der Gnostiker*", in *Zeitschrift für die neutestamentliche Wissenschaft*, vol. II, 1901.

Lipsius, Richard Adelbert, *Die Apokryphen Apostelgeschichten und Apostellegenden*, Braunschweig, 1883-1890.

——, et Maximilian Bonnet, *Acta Apostolorum Apocrypha*, vol. I, Leipzig, 1891.

Nestle, Eberhard and Erwin, *Novum Testamentum Graece*, 20. Aufl., Stuttgart, 1950.

Patrologiae Cursus Completus, Series Graeco-Latina, published by J. P. Migne (= PG).

Patrologiae Cursus Completus, Series Latina, published by J. P. Migne (= PL).

Pauly-Wissowa-Kroll, *Realenzyklopädie der Klassischen Altertumswissenschaft*, 1898 f. (= PW).

Prophylaeum ad Acta Sanctorum Decembris, Brussels, 1940 (an annotated *Martyrologium Romanum*).

Redpath, Henry A.: see Hatch, Edwin.

Schimmelpfeng, Georg: see Hennecke, *Handbuch*.

Schermann, Theodor, *Prophetarum Vitae Fabulosae Indices Apostolorum Discipulorumque Domini Dorotheo-Epiphanio-Hippolyto Allisque Vindicata* in *Bibliotheca Scriptorum Graecorum et Romanorum Teubneriana*, Leipzig, 1907.

——, *Propheten- und Apostellegenden nebst Jüngerkatalogen, Texte und Untersuchungen*, vol. XXXI, part. 3, Leipzig, 1907.

Schmoller, Alfred, *Handkonkordanz zum griechischen Neuen Testament*, 8. Aufl., Stuttgart, 1949.

Stegmüller, Fridericus, *Repertorium Biblium Medii Aevi*, vol. I, Madrid, 1950 (falsely written MCMXL on title page). This is a complete bibliography of Biblic and Apocryphal writings, replacing Delehaye.

Swete, Henry B., *The Old Testament in Greek*, Cambridge, 1890 f.

Von Gutschmidt, Alfred, *Kleine Schriften*, vol. II, Leipzig, 1890 includes reprint of "Die Königsnamen in den apokryphen Apostelgeschichten", *Rheinisches Museum für Philologie*, Neue Folge, vol. XIX, 1864.

Vögel, Heinrich Joseph, *Grundriss der Einleitung in das Neue Testament*, Münster, 1925.

Walker, Williston, *A History of the Christian Church*, New York, 1918.

Wright, William, *Apocryphal Acts of the Apostles*, 2 vols., London, 1871.

Quispel, G., "An Unknown Fragment of the Acts of Andrew", *Vigiliae Christianae*, X, 3-4, 1956, pp. 129-148.